GUIDED MEDITATION

Guided Meditation for Sleep, Relaxation & Stress Relief

(Guided Meditation for Overcoming Stress and Anxiety)

Bonnie Cruz

Published by Alex Howard

Bonnie Cruz

All Rights Reserved

Guided Meditation: Guided Meditation for Sleep, Relaxation & Stress Relief (Guided Meditation for Overcoming Stress and Anxiety)

ISBN 978-1-77485-071-8

All rights reserved. No part of this guide may be reproduced in any form without permission in writing from the publisher except in the case of brief quotations embodied in critical articles or reviews.

Legal & Disclaimer

The information contained in this book is not designed to replace or take the place of any form of medicine or professional medical advice. The information in this book has been provided for educational and entertainment purposes only.

The information contained in this book has been compiled from sources deemed reliable, and it is accurate to the best of the Author's knowledge; however, the Author cannot guarantee its accuracy and validity and cannot be held liable for any errors or omissions. Changes are periodically made to this book. You must consult your doctor or get professional medical advice before using any of the suggested remedies, techniques, or information in this book.

Upon using the information contained in this book, you agree to hold harmless the Author from and against any damages, costs, and expenses, including any legal fees potentially resulting from the application of any of the information provided by this guide. This disclaimer applies to any damages or injury caused by the use and application, whether directly or indirectly, of any advice or information presented, whether for breach of contract, tort, negligence, personal injury, criminal intent, or under any other cause of action.

You agree to accept all risks of using the information presented inside this book. You need to consult a professional medical practitioner in order to ensure you are both able and healthy enough to participate in this program.

Table of Contents

INTRODUCTION 1

CHAPTER 1 : IMPORTANCE OF MEDITATION 6

CHAPTER 2: MEDITATION 14

CHAPTER 3: THE MEDITATION OF THE SUN 25

CHAPTER 4: HOW TO MEDITATE 34

CHAPTER 5: WHY PRACTICE SLEEP MEDITATION? 58

CHAPTER 6: MEDITATION HELPS YOU CREATE MORE HARMONIOUS, LOVING RELATIONSHIPS 65

CHAPTER 7: MOVING DEEPER 79

CHAPTER 8: A WALK TO THE BEACH AT SUNRISE 89

CHAPTER 9: SECOND WEEK OF MEDITATIONS 96

CHAPTER 10: EXPLORING THE PRACTICE OF MEDITATION 136

CHAPTER 11: RELAXATION AND STRESS SCRIPTS 143

CHAPTER 12: BREATHING MEDITATION 159

CONCLUSION 191

Introduction

The conscious mind is being utilized when you are awake to work, communicate with people, make decisions, and perform other day-to-day activities. While the conscious mind is only the outer surface of our thought process, it is the subconscious mind that is filing away the main information, which is embedded in it almost forever. It is humanly impossible for us to try and absorb everything at a conscious level. Our minds would be overloaded.

Think of it this way. Throughout the day, as we interact with people and perform our tasks, the subconscious mind is collecting, sorting, and storing information for the future.

Sometimes you are searching for an important thing all over the place but can't find it. You give up hope of finding it. However, suddenly on an impulse, you look for it in a place where you wouldn't usually keep it. And bingo, there it is! How did you know it was where you found it? The knowledge of where it was kept had been in your subconscious mind all along. However, only when it communicated with your conscious mind, did you know where to find it.

Ever wondered what a "hunch" a "gut feeling" or "intuition" is? Often, it is nothing but a signal or communication from the subconscious mind to the conscious mind. Why are you asked to "sleep on your problems?" Simply because when we are asleep, our subconscious mind is most active.

When your subconscious' activity is at its peak, you can get some of the best insights and solutions to your problems simply because it holds information that is not accessible to our conscious mind. Some of our best solutions and "eureka" moments happen when we are asleep.

Has it happened several times that you've gone to bed thinking deeply about a problem with no solution in sight and suddenly you wake up with a solution and ask yourself why you hadn't thought of this before? It is your subconscious communicating with the conscious.

When you learn to reprogram your subconscious mind through meditation and positive thinking, you unlock or unleash the treasures or potential that have been held inside it for long. You can also use the power of meditation to restructure the imprints created in your subconscious mind during the early years of your life.

Whether your goal is to lose weight, stop smoking, overcome addictions, get rid of a phobia, develop greater confidence, or anything similar –you can use the power of meditation and positive thinking to manifest positive life goals.

Meditation is one of the best ways to unlock the power of the subconscious and deepen the connection between conscious and subconscious. The deep sense of relaxation brought about by meditation facilitates filtering out distracting thoughts and allows you to concentrate only on the subconscious. When you allow a fresh lease of positive thoughts into the subconscious mind, negative information is replaced by more constructive thoughts and ideas. The mind is relaxed and receptive, open to assimilating positive information to replace negative imprints that have been accumulated over a period of time.

It won't be achieved overnight. However, with consistent and disciplined practice, you will be able to successfully reprogram the subconscious to hold thoughts, ideas, and information that hold a positive purpose in your life. You are slowly able to break the control of negative thoughts over your actions and let positive thoughts rule.

Research has proven that meditation possesses the ability to alter our brain waves. This increases the accessibility of your subconscious mind, letting you reprogram it to meet your goals.

Take a bunch of successful people from different fields and carefully notice what they have in common with each other. One of the things that will stand out is their thoughts or beliefs. They have successfully empowered themselves with virtues such as will-power, self-control, persistence, and discipline.

There is an inner drive that pushes them to accomplish their goals. Our subconscious mind is the potent inner drive that helps unlock our true potential. There are plenty of people who are equally, if not more talented, that these successful people. However, not everyone enjoys their level of success. Why? Simply because successful people have mastered the unlocking of their true potential through the power of their thoughts or mind!

Meditation is the key to unlocking the power of your subconscious mind and using it to fulfill your dreams.

Chapter 1 : Importance Of Meditation

Some people love to suggest meditation as a means to help with issues in life. Why is that? what's so crucial about meditation? Well, that's what this chapter will help with. In this, you'll learn about the importance of meditation and why it is essential to help with negative thoughts and anxiety.

So, what is It?

Meditation is an ancient practice, used to help control your mind, and from this, your own life, and help you discover yourself. It's an excellent way to help you get control over your mind, to take out any negative issues that might be in your head.

Have you ever been so anxious that you feel like you have no energy, but can't sleep, or you feel like your thoughts are making you go crazy?

Well, the best part about it is that meditation can help you with this. You'll be able to eliminate the negative thoughts, anxiety, worries, and stress that are preventing you from truly living life.

Meditation, on a regular basis, can help to mitigate the instances of both stress, and anxiety to help you feel better. You're essentially feeling mentally and physically fresh, especially when you're dealing with stressful situations.

Do you need to be religious? You might wonder if you need to be Buddhist, Hindu, or practice any sort of religion. The answer is no. lots of times, people think meditation is just sitting there, saying the word "ohm" for hours on end in the lotus sitting position, but that's actually not the case. Meditation can be used to help relax, and it can help you to learn how to harness your issues so that you feel physically and mentally free in order to help make your life even better for you as well.

Meditation can be used when you feel well, and if you want to feel better about stressful situations. The big thing to remember is that you don't even need a reason to meditate. Even if you're feeling good, being able to meditate can help make you feel better, and in a sense, it's kind of a preventative measure when it comes to health issues.

In the world of quick fix medications and advertisements, sometimes having that thrown in your face isn't what you need. Sometimes, the one thing that you do need, is a little bit of self-guided meditation, so that you can be okay with what you need to do, and in turn, you'll be able to harness better control over your life.

That isn't to say to forgo any and all medications. Of course not. But meditation can help you sort out a lot of the reasoning and feelings behind why you might feel anxious, and it allows you to practice self-reflection to understand better why you are responding the way that you are, and it also allows you to be more mindful in life.

Physical Benefits of Meditation

Physical benefits do happen with meditation. Now, it's not some magic pill that will help to lower your blood pressure or make headaches go away. If you need to pop an Ibuprofen because your headache is driving you up the wall, then pop that. But, it's also important to realize that you can couple this with traditional medicine in order to help you feel better in life and to help you alleviate a lot of the tensions and issues there.

For example, meditation can help with physical tension, and get rid of psychosomatic issues caused by tension. So, if you're stressed and you're so tense, you've got an insane pressure headache driving you mad, a little bit of meditation can help with that.

It also helps to be prophylaxis against stress, so if you start to feel like you're wound up and stressed, this is one of the best ways to prevent it from driving you further up the wall.

It does work in a physical sense as well. Your blood pressure is affected by stress, and that's something you want to keep low, because high blood pressure can lead to heart conditions, including a heart attack, but with meditation, you can lower it to a controllable level so that you feel more at ease, and you're not out of sorts. It also will strengthen the immune system. Think about it, when we are stressed for hours and hours on end, we are going to suffer from a compromised immune system, and that's not fun. But, with meditation, you can start to eliminate these problems, and you'll be stronger.

It also plays a part in your general life. The aging process can be markedly slowed down by this. If you feel like you just see wrinkles upon wrinkles, maybe a little bit of meditation can help. Lots of times, we put so much stress on our bodies, which is how we end up aging so much, but with a little bit of meditation, you can actually shave a few years of aging off your body, and you'll look, and feel so much better than you did before.

Finally, it's an excellent way to recharge our batteries. It's refreshing, makes us feel good, and we can ultimately feel better than we did before, and in turn, we'll be able to really reduce the pain and issues that we are dealing with, and it's definitely a nice, added benefit.

So yes, it isn't just a simple mental exercise, but it's also a physical exercise that can ultimately help you as a person get the most out of your life, and really make you feel good.

Meditation can make you happier

Meditation is also super important because you can lead a happier life. Studies have shown that those who meditate tend to live happier lives than those that do otherwise. That's because, meditation can make the flow of constructive thoughts and emotions better, and even a few minutes meditating can make a difference. There is also scientific evidence that shows that Buddhist monks were much happier when they meditated, and that's due to the prefrontal cortex being much more active, which means that they were much happier as a result.

This also plays into how you handle anxiety, stress, and depression, both of which are actually major psychological issues in the brain. Those that have their stress regulators controlled with meditation tend to be less depressed. So, if you meditate more, you're going to be less depressed, and you'll also reduce the stress and anxiety, two other common factors found with depression. This is because, when you focus on the experiences within each moment, you learn to remain calm, even in the worst of situations, and it also can reduce the instance of anxiety in the body, since you'll be able to handle the future better, and with less uncertainty. This means you'll be much calmer, and much happier as a result of your actions. It does make a significant difference in how you handle the stress of life and the different means to make it easier for you, and you'll be able to, with meditation, handle the ways of life that you may not have been able to in the past way better than before. So yes, it does work, and it can help you experience a better, more fulfilling existence.

Immediate help, immediate benefits

The benefits that you get from meditation aren't something that you are going to have to work on for months on end. In fact, you can actually feel these benefits extremely quickly, once you start meditating. The calmness, peace of mind, and the feeling of happiness, even though subtle and fleeting, does happen. You'll be able to experience these benefits immediately, regardless of any issues that you might have before. It may make you think that your mind will be busier than ever before, but that's not the case. In fact, it can help you fall asleep even faster than you did before, so it's worth it.

Meditation is so important, and it can help with stress, anxiety and the like, so don't be afraid to get the help that you need from this and start to relax your mind today!

Chapter 2: Meditation

Meditation has a long history chiefly in the Buddhism tradition. In India, meditation dates back to more than 5000 years. Between 2000 and 3000 BC, discoveries of Vedic Meditation texts on Hindu texts increased the interest in meditation. During the 1000 BC, ancient Indians found the Qi Gong, which was a meditative motion that later became Tai Chi. The development of Buddhism in 588 BC is attributable to Buddha's meditation. From the Buddhism notion, meditation is a technique that seeks to free the mind from any suffering. The men who introduced the practice are the yogis. They meditated as a way to train their bodies and minds to achieve wellness. One of the Indian Yogis, known as Patanjali, defined meditation as a process of self-realization. Pantajali wrote the yoga techniques applicable today, with the seventh stage being meditation. Meditation paved the way for Yoga, which continued to spread gradually in China, Tibet, and India.

In the West, the monks were the first people to meditate, which was 200 AC. The monks practiced meditation as a way to grower closer to God. Later on, several Jewish groups meditated regularly to grow spiritually. In the 1500s, St. Theresa favored the practice of meditation, and it grew extensively during that period. However, the Christian religion did not embrace the concept entirely. The growth of meditation in the U.S mostly gained precedence in the 1800s when Asian priests presented the ideas on meditation during a religious leaders' meeting. Later in the 1960s, the Beatles started practicing meditation leading to the rapid growth of the practice in the West. In recent years, meditation is gaining full acceptance in science and healthcare. More people are viewing it trendy and as a part of mental detox. Resultantly, millions of young and older people have been meditating, not only as a stress-reliever but also for relaxation.

So, what is meditation? In simple terms, meditation is the concept of being peaceful, silent, and meditative. Buddha once said meditation is when a mirror does not reflect anything. The Latin words, meditari, which is to think and mederi, which is to heal, make up the word meditation. Originally, meditation is from the Sanskrit term 'Medha,' meaning wisdom. It also has origins from the phrase shamatha, meaning relaxation or calmness. From the two derivations, it is clear that meditation makes your mind quiet, leading one to have contact with the self or true identity.

Consequently, you will experience bliss, peace, and joy. Through meditation, you understand your mind and learn ways to transform any negative thoughts into positive thoughts. For successful meditation, you will need to have attitudes such as patience, trust, non-judgmental, letting go, and acceptance.

Scientifically, research on medication was evident in 1963. James Funderburk created a collection of studies on meditation under the guidance of Swami Rama. In fact, western scientists studied Swami Rama as the first yogis. While scientists had concluded that most of the bodily processes are involuntary, Rama proved them otherwise. He demonstrated his innate abilities to control some of his physical processes voluntarily. Rama controlled some of the processes, such as body temperature, blood pressure, and heartbeat. Through meditation, he could change his heartbeat while in a motionless posture. Rama could also use his mind to contract and dilate his blood vessels, consequently affecting his skin temperatures. Further, Rama could get his brain to a deep sleep while he remained conscious of his surroundings. Many of his demonstrations triggered the scientific community to study more about meditation and its impacts on the body.

In the decades that followed, scientific studies increased in quality and quantity. Practitioners within other traditions such as the Tibetan Lamas and the Zen monks demonstrated and studied the processes of mind over the body. In the 1970s, Dr. Herbert Benson studied the impact of meditation at Harvard University. His contribution enhanced the acknowledgment of meditation in healthcare. In the 21st century, meditation has mostly become a secularized concept. However, spiritual meditation is still in existence, especially in Hinduism. The wide-ranging benefits on overall wellness, mind, and body are attributable to the increasing popularity of meditation.

Recently, meditation has become more prevalent in stress management and enhancement of mindfulness. Meditation cultivates mindfulness. It involves having an awareness of your mind at a particular moment. During meditation, you might experience disruptive thoughts, but the process allows you to let them go. With a clear mind, you can embrace new ideas and perspectives. As such, you get new ways of handling stressful situations, among other issues. While meditation hails predominantly in India, the concept is devoid of Buddhism. Individuals have a mindful nature, and meditation ranks as one of the essentials of human capacity. Mindfulness allows people to have fewer reactions to external happenings. The situation creates attention that helps to clear the mind, generate energy, and promote joy.

The process of meditation is three-fold, leading to a consciousness state that brings about clarity and serenity. The first stage is dealing with our 'normal' mind, which is, in reality, abnormal. The reason one can view the mind as strange is the uncontrolled reaction to sensory stimuli. Bouncing from thoughts to thoughts is the nature of almost all humans of sound mind. As discussed in the introduction, our minds are like rooms full of clamoring monkeys, the noise and the jumping up and down define how our thoughts are structured. This simple diagram is an actual illustration of our rational minds at every moment.

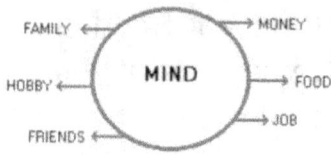

The second phase of meditation is concentration, which is the gradual process of gaining control of the mind. Concentration involves picking a subject or an object and focusing on it exclusively without diversifying your mind. Without active attention, meditation is impossible. The illustration below is that of a concentrating mind.

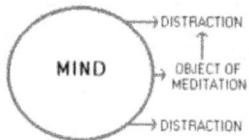

The last stage is meditation, characterized by unbroken attention. When you concentrate without distractions, the concentration on the meditation object deepens spontaneously and effortlessly.

At this final stage, your mind unites with the object of meditation. You get to the contemplation stage, which is the state of utmost consciousness. Being in a state of consciousness 'separates' us from the rest of the universe. Initially, this deep sense of peace might be challenging to achieve. You will need to practice the procedures repeatedly and slowly to achieve the serenity you desire.

The process of meditation is dependent on a few aspects that play a crucial role in the determination of how effective the eventual outcomes. When preparing for meditation, one needs to consider the immediate environment as a critical factor towards achieving the desired end goal. Meditation is most effective when in a serene, quiet surrounding away from the distractions of life. The process of preparing for meditation may require a keen focus on the calmness of the surroundings and the comfort within which the body and mind can enter into a space of complete relaxation. If in a room, ensure that the place is well-ventilated to allow for the circulation of fresh air into the room. Breathing is a critical part of the process of meditation, which means that a ventilated setting is a necessity.

The other option would be to enroll in a yoga studio, where such factors are often put into consideration. Then decide on which techniques work best for you.

This book offers a wide range of techniques to determine from before deciding on what works best. You may need to engage a meditation specialist if unsure of what may work best for you. The next critical consideration should be the consideration of how to undertake specific movements and postures when engaging in the meditation process. Essentially, it is worth noting that particular positions and movement may require extreme stretches, which may lead to injuries if not well-choreographed. Understanding the choreography in each of the poses and motions will also enhance the possibility of achieving the best results from the meditation process. Consulting a specialist before beginning the process may be useful, especially when engaging in the highly physical meditation techniques such as Yoga. On the same note having a YouTube tutorial or other sources of information can help you begin the process of meditation from the point of knowledge.

People must understand that meditation is not an escapist approach when faced with challenges. In fact, it is the opposite; meditation allows you to confront problems and to demystify any misconceptions about a situation. It mainly involves settling one experience in an objective way to achieve a calm state of mind. With the many complexities in the modern society, meditation can be an ideal solution. The process is straightforward because the object of meditation can be anything. You only need to be away from distractions and focus on concentration.

If you want to start the practice of meditation today, thousands of online guides can prove resourceful. You only need whether you are a beginner or an expert in meditation; the different guides have stipulated minutes to help your mind relax. Furthermore, you can meditate successfully without following specific guides. You will only need a quiet place, the right posture, and an object of meditation.

Chapter 3: The Meditation Of The Sun

This second meditation is highly suggested to everyone that suffers from anxiety and stress. During this session you will be able to quickly and easily relieve any negative thought that is afflicting you right now. How is that possible? Because this type of meditation is a natural anxiety cure that will allow you to gain control over some of your body's automatic responses to stressful situations.

This easy meditation technique (as every other technique presented in this book) can be used any time, any place, to relieve anxiety and reduce stress. I suggest you to listen to this guided meditation while laying down in your bed or sitting comfortably on the sofa at the end of a busy day: you are going to feel refreshed and at peace once you complete the meditation.

Let's get started!

Find a comfortable, relaxed and balanced position. Give yourself permission to be completely present for yourself, and let your body and mind calm down until they become soft and relaxed.

Breathe in, feel relaxed...
breathe out, feel calm...
Breathe in, feel relaxed...
breathe out, feel calm...
Breathe in, feel relaxed...
breathe out, feel calm...
Breathe in, feel relaxed...
breathe out, feel calm...

Allow the mind to distance itself from all thoughts and orientate awareness on your breath. Breathe naturally and do not force a specific rhythm. Let your breath come and go.

Carefully, now, drive your attention from the breath to the space in which you are.

Feel the energy and atmosphere of this space as it permeates all of your being. Notice the noises in the background. Maybe there is a clock ticking, maybe there are cars passing just outside your

windows. Whatever you feel it is fine, let your attention rest on the external.
Breathe in, feel relaxed...
breathe out, feel calm...
Breathe in, feel relaxed...
breathe out, feel calm...
Breathe in, feel relaxed...
breathe out, feel calm...
Breathe in, feel relaxed...
breathe out, feel calm...
Now bring the attention back to the breath. Take your time and you will naturally reach a place of warmth and ease. Stay in this state where you feel your body and mind completely calm, relaxed and full of peace for a few minutes, without letting go the focus on your breath.
Breathe in, feel relaxed...
breathe out, feel calm...
Breathe in, feel relaxed...
breathe out, feel calm...
Breathe in, feel relaxed...
breathe out, feel calm...
Breathe in, feel relaxed...
breathe out, feel calm...

Breathe in, feel relaxed...
breathe out, feel calm...
Breathe in, feel relaxed...
breathe out, feel calm...
Breathe in, feel relaxed...
breathe out, feel calm...
Breathe in, feel relaxed...
breathe out, feel calm...
Now, begin to scan your body from the bottom of your toes up to the top of your head. Do this slowly and stop on each part of your body to listen to what it has to tell you. If you feel contracted on a specific area, keep the attention on that part for as long as you feel it relaxing. It is important that you do not force this process, just keep breathing and you will feel your body getting more and more relaxed.
Up from your feet to your pelvic floor.
Breathe in, feel relaxed...
breathe out, feel calm...
Breathe in, feel relaxed...
breathe out, feel calm...
Breathe in, feel relaxed...
breathe out, feel calm...
Breathe in, feel relaxed...

breathe out, feel calm...
Keep going up, reaching your chest and your shoulders. This is where a lot of tension can be usually found, so take your time in this area.
Breathe in, feel relaxed...
breathe out, feel calm...
Breathe in, feel relaxed...
breathe out, feel calm...
Breathe in, feel relaxed...
breathe out, feel calm...
Breathe in, feel relaxed...
breathe out, feel calm...
And finally you reach your head. Keep breathing into your head and feel the air slowly filling every empty space of your head. Keep breathing, the sun is rising.
Breathe in, feel relaxed...
breathe out, feel calm...
Breathe in, feel relaxed...
breathe out, feel calm...
Breathe in, feel relaxed...
breathe out, feel calm...
Breathe in, feel relaxed...
breathe out, feel calm...
Breathe in, feel relaxed...

breathe out, feel calm...
Breathe in, feel relaxed...
breathe out, feel calm...
In your own time, try to imagine a sphere of liquid sunlight just a few inches above your head. Imagining a small sun can be beneficial during this part, as it helps your mind and body to adapt to this new entity. With every breath now, feel the liquid sunlight coming down into your head and through your spine, reaching the bottom of your feet through your pelvic floor and legs. Your body is getting filled with this warm and soft light. Can you feel it?

If you are struggling, it is fine, do not force it too much. It will get better over time.

Breathe in, feel relaxed...
breathe out, feel calm...
Breathe in, feel relaxed...
breathe out, feel calm...
Breathe in, feel relaxed...
breathe out, feel calm...
Breathe in, feel relaxed...
breathe out, feel calm...
Breathe in, feel relaxed...
breathe out, feel calm...

Breathe in, feel relaxed...
breathe out, feel calm...
Breathe in, feel relaxed...
breathe out, feel calm...
Breathe in, feel relaxed...
breathe out, feel calm...
The liquid sunlight is filling every inch of your body and is taking away all the anxiety and stress of the day. Keep breathing, I will give you a few more minutes to stay in this state as the liquid sunlight is purifying your body and soul.
Breathe in, feel relaxed...
breathe out, feel calm...
Breathe in, feel relaxed...
breathe out, feel calm...
Breathe in, feel relaxed...
breathe out, feel calm...
Breathe in, feel relaxed...
breathe out, feel calm...
Breathe in, feel relaxed...
breathe out, feel calm...
Breathe in, feel relaxed...
breathe out, feel calm...
Breathe in, feel relaxed...
breathe out, feel calm...

Breathe in, feel relaxed...
breathe out, feel calm...
Breathe in, feel relaxed...
breathe out, feel calm...
Breathe in, feel relaxed...
breathe out, feel calm...
Breathe in, feel relaxed...
breathe out, feel calm...
Breathe in, feel relaxed...
breathe out, feel calm...
Breathe in, feel relaxed...
breathe out, feel calm...
Breathe in, feel relaxed...
breathe out, feel calm...
Breathe in, feel relaxed...
breathe out, feel calm...
Breathe in, feel relaxed...
breathe out, feel calm...

Now bring the attention back to the body and start feeling your arms and legs once again. You can close your hands or move your fingers, just to take control of the space around you.

Please, keep the eyes closed for now and enjoy the beautiful moment you are living.

You have given yourself the time to feel better and that is absolutely incredible.
Breathe in, feel relaxed...
breathe out, feel calm...
Breathe in, feel relaxed...
breathe out, feel calm...
Breathe in, feel relaxed...
breathe out, feel calm...
Breathe in, feel relaxed...
breathe out, feel calm...
Now become aware of the environment around you once again. Feel the different sounds, the temperature of the room you are in and once you are ready, open the eyes again.

Chapter 4: How To Meditate

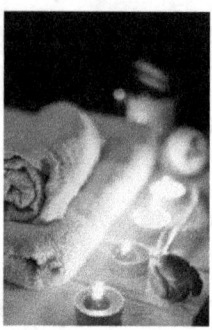

Figure 3: Free Credits

Preliminary Instructions

Meditation cannot be theoretical, like how a customer will not satisfy his hunger by going through the restaurant menu. You have to eat to be full. Meditation will prove to be a treasure if an individual can refer to the works of the past. Those instruments of the past can give some insights into the instruction on how to expound.

Let us pay some critical look to these instructions:

Preliminary instructions and general advice

Let us look now at some of these teachings.

Motivation:

As far as action is concerned, we can begin by a specific meditation, but our motives should come into account. Our motivations, could it be self-centered or limited- that will give us the exact path to heed, and we will do some determinant factors.

Everyone deserves to be stress-free and gain some happiness, and those are our inborn rights. But what we make as a resolution can falter or be conflicting with our aspirations most of the time. We do search for happiness in places is lacking, and we resort to sad situations that buttress us with disturbance. Conventional wisdom has it that we do not have to abandon what seems goodness in life. Miseries have to be brushed off but are always with us as our dear friends. Mental confusion can dim out judgment and clarity, but we can cure this confusion by facing reality and transit our minds. It can end our sufferings, spiritual toxins, aggressiveness, greediness, pride, and jealousy. These are the lethal poisons that come due to self-centeredness and elevated ego.

There different forms of suffering: they are, the pain we can see, sickness, ravages of wars, tragedies, and earthquakes. There is also unseen suffering relating to impermanence and can disguise itself inform of superficial contentment.

Another profound aspect of suffering comes from our deep-seated ignorance. It stays with us if we do not act on our delusional grip and selfishness pleasure. The truth is, even though life can most of the times seem enjoyable, events can get worse. For example, going to a get-together, pleasurable picnic and being attacked by marauding lions. But an even more severe disease that lurks in us comes from our inward ignorance. If we don't get out of that cocoon, the delusional grip will haunt us and selfishness as well, and mental affliction will continue to agonize us. It causes endless sufferings. In this respect, a life lived through unnecessary ignorance is not at all deemed as a happy one.

There are some noble truths about suffering:

That we should act and know is the time to leave the strain and the bondage of suffering. Secondly, we should understand that pains have causes, ignorance being the culprit, obsessiveness, hatred, and more toxic feelings. Whereas these sufferings can be evaded or eliminated, suffering can get done away. Eventually, there is the fourth one about the same feel bad scenario that we should not only fancy ending our problems but those who are available to us.

Humans are creatures who interdepend on each other. The excellent price any reasonable person should aim is to liberate others from mental and physical slavery. You can also improve on their wellbeing. The portions of this book about meditation are convenient and more concise to those who want to achieve better results in meditation. Using them in one's session of meditation interpretively will enhance ones mental capacities as the day goes along.

Meditation: A Vow to Transform

Take a reality check on what sort of person are you. Is there any are you find yourself with some shortcomings and you need to improve? Mirror yourself. Can you see the will power to change? Make a determination to achieve knowing that nothing changes if we cannot raise our heads above the water. Can see you being the giant of change as the time and the clock tick? Make a vow to aim at transforming yourself and targeting how you can dispel the pains of others like you who are searching for the light in the murkiness of the tunnel. As a general rule, we should not wish to make efforts to be determined to achieve and succeed.

Sources of Inspiration

So are we dealing with the real issue or we are grappling with only some specific matters? Are our mental sights long term or shorter ones? Do we have ill motives or are purely based on compassion? Are our passions and compassion strictly bordered on family circles and friends? So to discover the true nature of oneself through thoughts and emotion s that is where to start --

Conditions Conducive To Meditation Practice

The Advice of a Qualified Guide

The starting point is, know the ways to heed what to discard as rubbish traits, and getting a competent adviser into this is not bad at all. In best of all cases, he will prove to be a trove of advice to you and inspiration. It is because of being into the game for so many years. Nothing came to override the power of working beside a master. The knowledge one can impart is a lot and inexhaustible, his presence and teaching with constancy makes the one learning not to get fed up quickly or get sidetracked.

Maybe masters are elusive on your side, but you can tap the advice of those with know-how and experience. Then it would be advisable to borrow some information from the tremendous conventional wisdom of contemplative thinkers. If that is not at your reach either, is you can vigorously do some research from reliable sources of the same.

A Suitable Place for Meditation

Our minds, time, and where about are most of the times overtaken by activities or preoccupations without end. So, in the beginning, we should set out favorable conditions. Eventually, the effects of meditation will catch up within us, but as a beginner, we need more solace, a protected environment which to train our mental powers.

In high seas, you cannot learn to navigate a ship through the stormy waters, but the good weather on a calm sea will be okay. So similarly meditation thrives best in the environment with quietness where the mind can come into grips with clarity.

Comparisons have got likened to this atmosphere as an oil lamp. If the flaming fire gets exposed to the wind, the light might fail, and there is likability of being blown out. But if the flame is shielded from the wind, it will not go off. In the same manner, if our minds get shielded from the distractions coming from the other side, mindfulness gets the new lease of life. It becomes more stable and acts with clarity and precision even though some natural distractions are inevitable.

Appropriate Physical Posture

Most of the times Your physical position upsets your mental wellbeing .chances are that if assume that is too much relaxed, your meditativeness can wallow into tiredness. If you think a demeanor that is too carefree, primarily if you lie down, the likelihood are that your meditation will wandering into drowsiness. Too stiff and edgy position can steer us into mental agitation. There are seven points of posture, and these are:

The legs ought to be crossed, mainly referred to as lotus posture. First, you do by right leg over the left one, then vice versa.

Hands should rest palms go up, The hands rest palms up, on the segment in the posture of composure, and right hand on the left one and the thumb tips should touch each other. With the right hand on top of the left, and the tips of the thumbs touching each other. A distinction is allowing the hands break flat, palms down, on the knees.

Shoulders must be balanced, giving space between upper arms and torso as well making the chest open and relaxed paving for more breath.

The spinal cord should also be like a straightened metal bar.

The jaw is popped in, somewhat toward the throat.

The direction of the tongue dashes the palate, near the front teeth.

Eyes must be open widely or slightly closed; the look should be focusing ahead of the nose.

If the cross-legged pose is daunting, sitting on a chair could suffice. Any raised platform can also do. The aim is to maintain an equilibrium position. Do this with straightened back part of the body. Rumor has it that if the body is straight, the energy does not get crooked and the mind will be more harmonious.

It is feasible to adjust your position regarding your meditation. If you have inclinations to get into sleep on the process, you can raise your torso and do vigorous posture and your face upward. If the mind gets tired, you can relax a bit and then gaze downward. Maintaining a suitable position for long is advantageous, even if it feels not comfortable, you can relax, then you go back to the required posture. You can also direct your attention to the unpleasant pain without magnifying it. Deal with it like how you would react to any other sensation or pleasant or not because that is part and parcel of your mindfulness. Also alternating meditation with sitting, walking, and so forth it can be up building.

Your Enthusiasm as the Driving Force behind Perseverance

For someone to get the benefits of any endeavor, interest matters most. Considering the outcomes in advance will make the meditation more endurable, not just a harrowing situation, and the interest can increase as well. But that does not put the reflection as very simple and pleasant. Majority of those who did immerse themselves into it they have labeled it as non-pleasant expedition, not an entertainment. A trek to the high hills is not an easy task and fun; there are hardships, exhaustion, high altitudes, or giving up along the way. The main thing one can do is not to give up but cultivating more interest, zeal, and determination .so that will invigorate someone who feels like calling it off. Their s satisfaction if someone achieves a specific goal they have set to aim at no matter how tough it is.

Some General Advice

It is crucial to retain the constancy of contemplation day after day because, in this way, your practice increasingly earnings substance and stability. Like the small gush of water little by little can make a stream and then the vast river. It is better to meditate regularly, repeatedly with short span s of times than long ones which can weigh you down. Perform like the twenty minutes, each day then break. Formally, take advantage of short breaks in your daily activities to recall the experience you had during your last sessions for a moment.

Brief, repeated sessions have a better impact than protracted long ones they can enhance the next continuity. For a fledgling plant to get nurtured well, it has to get watered every time. You do not need to rush this process. Meditation is a process that should always be gradual, not a very sudden and weighty application that can overwhelm your mind.

When you meditate sporadically, chances are you may relapse to your old habits. You need to avoid this if you do not want to remain a victim of anxiety and negative emotions. The best way you could prevent these emotions is to meditate frequently.

Being diligent does not mean relying on personal mood or outside triggers. If it is irritating to meditate, enjoyable, or not comfortable, the only essential ingredient is to persevere. If you fail during the session then is not the wrong meditation, it is you who has the shortcomings, and so vigorous training is needed. Moreover, it is when you feel like quitting that victory is around the corner, so cultivating resilience is the best policy into this.

Practitioners get admonished against placing too much emphasis on personal inner experiences that may come up during the meditation. Such a session could be in the form of ecstasy, inward emotions, or distant thoughts. They can render themselves like pleasing landscapes you could see while sitting pretty on a train. It would be unthinkable to get out the ride and assume to go and see them at a close range because your target was to reach your destination. In respect to meditation, the aim is to rise from within a while. And the product of your work can not be outstanding to everyone round the clock or even years, so due diligence is needed.

Hastily deeds cannot be compatible with meditation; any profound transformation has to take more time. It should not worry you how long it might take only the hint is, don't put unrealistic deadlines which can obstruct progress. The only precious advice is you should know from where you are hitting the road. You should also discern where to destine one, so the direction is what matters most as opposed to quick fixes.

Additionally progressing is not based on void pursuits, as one move on then one dot joins the other, and in the long run, a straight line gets made. But in the long term is also good to see you have made some progress, not just occasional experiences in a transient way.

Tuning the Mind toward Meditation

Stronger meditation comes as a result knowing these basics:

The valuableness of human existence

The delicateness of human lifespan and the fleeting nature of entirely every living thing

Picking beneficial schedules and shunning harmful engagements

The substandard quality integral in customary life

The Pricelessness of Human Life

If we enjoy conditions of freedom and opportunity, human life has extraordinary possibilities for inner development. By utilizing experience well, it can offer a chance to actualize and develop the best in us. But if we get tainted by ignorance and mental misappropriation, the treasure trove of life can remain out of our reachable point. But the basic things we require to emerge out of this dudgeon we must first work from this area of life. This part of life can get linked to the purification process of the gold whereby the precious nuggets get washed, and then they shine with utter brilliance.

Meditation: Precious Human Life

Grasping how worthwhile human life is and make it bring out outstanding qualities is a goal worth attaining. Contrary to animal kingdom livelihood, human capacity can reach the unthinkable heights. Human wisdom can create permanent benefits of existence or horrible tragedies of life .it can be used to be the machines of aiming to the sky, or eradicate the maladies of human suffering and the ethical consequences see the overall human happiness. Every moment of living has benefits, and like a planter who has prepared his fields, if he comes to the finality of his life, there are no feelings of soreness. The best of his ability persist for a few jiffies in the direction of profound gratefulness aroused by these examinations.

The Transitory Nature of All Things

What is the use of reflecting on the transitory nature of beings and things? Human life has an incalculable value, but it doesn't last forever. Thinking on the temporariness of life makes human realizes the importance of passing the time. Every moment counts and is precious. But the time is so fleeting that it goes so fast like gold dust between human fingers, subsequently, why do humans put off what is intuitive of the prime importance? There is no doubt that impatience will lead us to where we should not be or to get quick fixes if we do that our determinations are going to be in vain. We should not see our futures as if they are complete towards our perspectives. So in retrospect every moment of life is worthwhile, and death is guaranteed, and we could be living in this minute, and the next minute, we are gone away like a mist.

The way we reckon about the end of our lives can have a profound effect on our whole beings. Many people have morbid fear when they think about their sad ending in life. They do not understand how it can be their inner source of refreshment and inspiration. The death is inevitable, and men are born equal, and they die as similar no matter what they try to acquire in this uncertain and competitive world. The intelligent person perceives death as a means, not to an end but as a way of invigorating his courage and abandoning useless distractions. Such a person is unscarred by death, but he does not forget about the fragility of living. So, with this in mind, he cannot afford to lose track of where he comes and where he is heading. An intelligent person will always resort to better himself each passing moment. He also checks his weak areas, and in the general view, he can attain the elusive happiness. He can be in a position to go to the grave in tranquility for the sake of others.

We should realize the ever-changing condition of almost every living thing in this world but do we have the self-will to discern the fake and unnecessary items? Or can anything be permanently undesirable or hateful? How can we be positioned to understand that something belongs to us nor not?

How can we regard of a permanent character in the core of the continually changing torrent of our cognizance?

We should understand that change is inherently inevitable. In all things, whether they are inanimate or not animate, but the human has the inward phenomena to perceive everything as if it will last forever. But such feelings can backfire if we are stepping on the wrong footstool of the realty. Such defiance of clinging resolve sooner or well along translates into misery since it is unavailable of step with the trueness. Additionally, if change comes to happen, and we had prepared for it since the change has to happen and is usually the nature of all nonliving and living things. It is not going to be a drama.

Meditation: Make the Best Possible Use of Time

Think about the track of the seasons, the days and years, every time and the aspects which can detrimentally affect any living individual. Think about the reality of existence and getting old or dying. Unexpectedly, can anyone know how much is remaining before he can go to the land of sleep or in? Even if you live to be a hundred few years, your life cannot be counted as a well-lived life. It is because death is unavoidable. The most valuable part is when you are breathing. When you are living in this world, act with positivity in any aspect of life. Try to be fruitful as best as possible. In hindsight, if you want to touch the skies, don't relapse for your sake only. Involve those who are likeminded. They can benefit, and it will never be too late to start and improve on your side.

From the outset, many are haunted by the death-like how a gazelle escapes from a hunter. On the way, there are no regrets, and as a farmer, you will sit down and enjoy your accomplishments even if the rain failed some of the times.

Choosing Beneficial Actions and Avoiding Harming Actions

Can human life be utilized for the better part of it? But how can we do that because we are bound to be interrupted by the outside nuisances? But, if any undertaking has to succeed, you should do it with lots of insights and diligence. We can consider doing things and omitting others, depending on our motives. The sailor who sails at the high seas, the trekking guides and the craftsman who is very proficient with his work are all participants. They know that toiling at the moment on a whimsical level is there are no fruits at all. But if we get motivated by the goal we want to attain is, is more liberating from the purges of suffering. The aim is not to distinguish the evil and the right things, but to conform to the rules. The principles of right and wrongs are conventional. The only to make a list of ideas is acting with a precision, clear mind, and respects the portfolios of happiness and the sufferings we can discern if we are on the lookout enough. For example, if we want to avoid being incinerated by fire, we should run away from the flames.

Also, a hundred percent expectations do not suffice, and it is not a right and wise approach either. Our graceful and worst deeds cannot get predicted for sure. The limit we can do is exerting ourselves in any up building activity. Our motivations matter a lot. Our target is not to bring the benefits to ourselves but for others as well.

Meditation: Distinguishing the Causes of Happiness and Suffering

Letting your mindset in natural, ingenious harmony of clear thoughts is something of essence. Recognize how profoundly you can come out of the sufferings and steer yourself to the authenticity of happiness. To be concise, all humans have familiar or similar expectations or wishes. Most of those expectations get backed by greed, pride, ill feelings, and hatred. Although some of them when they get remedied can give out serenity, and wisdom and eventually contentment. There are some of the past contemporizes of knowledge. They understood it with insightfulness despite the occasional sufferings. Sometimes you can draw mental clear cut images of what you can do or not, and the perseverance can get attained in due courses of the time.

Sources of inspiration

Human beings always long to free themselves from the chains of misery. They follow gloom and pursue it .they long for joy but their stupidly decapitates it as what a warlord would do to his rival.

The Unsatisfactory Quality Inherent in ordinary life

We already decipher that our predicament is wanting and that transformation is not only an illusion to be pursued but desirable and possible. Obstacles and distractions are there. They will always be there; there are other disguises in our lives which can interfere with our lives in a seemingly attractive way. For instance, all time-consuming activities, immersive sensory actions, the constant pursuit of wealth, fame, and thirst for power. But agony is the most of all bound to happen will haunt us in the end. So facing the predicament on the face sternly, from the outset and root out the insignificant part of ills to us, we can genuinely derive happiness.

Meditation: Resolving to Change

In a short period, remember you are an individual, and you can change and realize your full potential. Whatever you are going through for a few moments, be aware of your potential for change. Whatever your current situation is, advancement and transformation are achievable. You can change how you view things and your wellbeing as well as drastically. A stable resolution to change is the best way to liberate yourself not even momentarily but for all times. First, arouse and ignite the perseverance needed and the feel-good qualities needed within you it is that they are latent.

Source of Inspiration

Exhausting your life's potential trying to attain secular goal like pleasures, fame, praise, -and the like is like fishing out the dry river bed. So having that in mind we should not aspire to pursue a useless course of life at all.

Chapter 5: Why Practice Sleep Meditation?

Profound sleep is a baffling state that we, for the most part, enter a few times every night. Its tendency is to some degree, less notable than the more emotional "dream rest." While we are exceptionally mindful today of dream rest, and of the capacity of certain individuals to be aware of and even direct their fantasies in a state known as clear dreaming, the nature of profound rest keeps on welcoming a feeling of a secret.

Sleep stages were first found during the 1930s when Loomis and his associates started doing expedite EEG accounts of dozing individuals. Phases of rest were perceived by the standard changes noted in the EEG.

By the late 1960s, it was conceivable to determine methods of dependably scoring these stages, and some information existed about their assumed job in the helpful procedure of rest. On account of the sensational idea of dreams and their chronicled job in religion, writing, and therapy, REM rest, during which these memorable encounters happen, turned out to be notable to the general population.

Less accentuation has been set on the non-dream condition of profound rest.

This phase of rest is otherwise called delta rest, slow-wave rest or, all the more as of late, N3. It is called delta rest in light of the nearness of high-abundancy, low-recurrence delta waves that are believed to happen in the EEG. Previously, this stage was isolated into two phases, stage 3 and stage 4, contingent upon the level of delta waves present. Stage 4 has a more prominent measure of delta wave action than stage 3, and was thought of as a more profound condition of rest. Research has not, be that as it may, had the option to plainly show any noteworthy contrast in the advantage of these two phases, and all the more as of late they have been consolidated into a solitary stage—N3.

Emotionally profound rest is a period of about complete withdrawal from nature. It is exceptionally hard to stir an individual in profound rest, and youngsters in this state might be about difficult to wake up.

It is from this phase sleepwalking rises. This happens when there is an abrupt excitement from profound rest that causes the engine habitats of the cerebrum—however not the higher focuses—to stir, so the individual is in a rest state separation described by complex engine action with constrained judgment and mindfulness.

Numerous significant physiological procedures happen during profound rest. Most profound rest happens during the initial two rest cycles, with the best measure of profound rest ordinarily happening in the principal cycle. As the night advances, profound rest diminishes and is supplanted by the lighter stage 2 rest and there is an expanding measure of REM rest toward morning. Profound rest is very powerful in diminishing the rest drive that fabricates consistently through the span of the day—definitely more viable than stage 2 rest in such manner.

One explanation that short evening snoozes of around 20 minutes may not influence evening time rest, while longer ones may bring about trouble nodding off, is that in a short rest, there isn't sufficient opportunity to cycle into profound rest; most rest is stage 2. On the off chance that N3 rest happens during a rest, it will quickly diminish your rest drive and make it difficult to nod off soon thereafter.

Human development hormone is discharged in beats during profound rest, and interference of this stage suddenly stops its discharge. The medication gamma hydroxybutyrate (GHB) was once utilized by jocks since it causes an expansion in profound rest. With this expansion in profound rest, there is additionally an arrival of development hormone. In grown-ups, development hormone advances cell fix that is essential after the pressure of weight preparing. Before, GHB was unreservedly accessible as an enhancement. Sadly, the capacity of this medication to instigate rest was abused by a few, who transformed it into a "date assault" tranquilize. It is presently firmly controlled and accessible just by remedy for treatment of clutters, for example, narcolepsy.

There are mental advantages of profound rest: By quickly lessening rest need, this phase of rest is a particularly reviving piece of the rest cycle, except if you are aroused out of it, in which case you will feel extremely drowsy and may encounter "rest inebriation," during which it is dangerous to drive. Some ongoing neural system look into additionally demonstrates that profound rest might be significant in helping clear the cerebrum for new learning the following day.

In some Eastern supernatural conventions, the condition of cognizance through which we normally experience the world is thought of as being one of gross mindfulness. There is a progressively unpretentious condition of mindfulness that might be created through contemplation and can be thought of as being increasingly inconspicuous and like that of the dreaming condition of cognizance.

The most profound degree of cognizance, in this plan, is the one wherein it is conceivable to get mindful of the vacancy in which all wonder are thought to happen. As per the basic savant Ken Wilber, it is conceivable, with preparing in cutting edge reflection, for individuals to know about the subtler conditions of awareness, including the conditions of dreaming and even profound rest.

Regardless of whether we know about the condition of profound rest, it capacities to reestablish us genuinely and intellectually. Tragically, our entrance to profound rest is additionally helpless against the impacts of pressure, rest interruption, maturing, and numerous medications. By forestalling satisfactory profound rest, these variables add to the summary sentiments that numerous individuals managing money related weight, rest apnea, maturing, or consuming certain medications experience every day.

What would we be able to do to get a greater amount of this grand, strangely therapeutic rest stage? There is no simple fix—we can't return to some time in the past on maturing, or dispense with life's omnipresent stressors. In any case, when we find a way to guarantee that we have a customary, pre-12 PM sleep time, that we get any apnea issue treated, and that we use unwinding breathing or other reflective strategies to slip into rest, we may without a doubt find that the strange and remedial forces of profound rest are inside our compass.

Chapter 6: Meditation Helps You Create More Harmonious, Loving Relationships

We all are aware that regular exercise has many health benefits for us. But without rest exercise would not be so benefic. The same goes for our mind. We spend all our time thinking, worrying, and we never give our mind a rest. Without allowing our mind some self healing time it may become exhausted. Same way as we need resting our bodies we also need to stop our thought process in order to rest our mind. Self-healing meditation is just that: allowing our mind time to rejuvenate and recover, resting the mind in silence.

Meditation is not about having no thoughts at all, which is a state difficult to achieve, but it is instead about just establishing a different connection with your thoughts. Instead of focusing our attention to whatever thought happens in our mind, in meditation we watch your thoughts from a different perspective. By regular practice of mediation you train yourself to focus your attention when and where you want. This is a very powerful skill that gives you the ability to control your mood and thoughts in more peaceful and productive directions. The clinical research has demonstrated in the recent years that this ability has profound self-healing benefits for our mental and physical health. The results of these studies into meditation are truly fascinating.

By studying the brainwaves of meditating people, the research found that the brain circuitry is different in those practicing meditation over a long-time. They have high brain activity especially in the area of the left prefrontal cortex, which is a region associated with positive mood and happiness. The studies also have shown that by the self healing power of mediation the brain can rewire itself.

We've all are aware about how stress can affect immunity and health. Many medical conditions are related to stress, such as ulcer, lower immunity, depression, heart disease, asthma, and diabetes. There is also scientific evidence that stress can shrinks neurons on the hippocampus, affecting our positive mood, memory, and learning capacity. However, the hippocampus has self healing capacity to regenerate and meditation reduces stress and activates this self healing ability. This is because meditation teaches us how to alter our responses to stress and increases the serotonin production, a neurotransmitter that influences sleep, mood, and appetite. Meditation is not only a way to relax, but also a precise strategy for health management and training the mind for emotional stability, increased power of observation and concentration.

In meditation, healing can happen because our calm, contented, and alert mind becomes like a very powerful laser beam. To achieve a perfect state of health, we need to remain emotionally stable, steady, and mentally calm. Health is not related to the body and the mind but, on a spiritual level is also connected with our consciousness. Health is a truly holistic state, involving all levels of body, mind, and soul.

Now the hard science has caught up with the oriental traditions thousands years old. Comprehensive scientific studies are showing that deep relaxation achieved through meditation changes our bodies on a genetic level. In long-term practitioners of relaxation methods such as meditation are activated more disease fighting genes compared to those who practiced no form of relaxation. In particular are switched on genes that protect from disorders such as cancers, high blood pressure, infertility, pain, and even rheumatoid arthritis. The changes are induced by what researches called "the relaxation effect", a phenomenon just as powerful as the medical drugs but without any negative side effects. The benefits of meditation increase with regular practice.

Meditation increases life energy

The oriental medicine and spiritual traditions go further in explaining the healing benefits of meditation. The vital life energy that is called prana, chi, or ki in different oriental traditions, is the very basis of our well being and health, for both mind and body. You can gain life energy through the regular practice of meditation. When your body is alive with more life energy, you feel full of good humor, energetic, and alert. On the other side, a lack of life energy results in poor enthusiasm, dullness, and lethargy.

Meditation dealing with illness

The oriental traditions consider that the root of an illness is in the mind. So, by clearing the mind of any disturbances the process of healing and recovery can speed up. Oriental traditional medicine considers that illnesses can develop from:

• Release of past impressions or Karma
• Imposed by nature: such as flu, common cold, and other epidemic
• Violation of natural law: such as lack of sleep or over-eating.

However, nature itself provides solutions for all these illnesses. By practicing meditation, the worries, stress, and anxieties are replaced by a positive state of mind, with positive impact on the brain and nervous system as well as on the physical body.

Because both health and illness are a part of the physical nature, it is advised you should not worry too much about it. You are giving more power to the illness when you worry about it. When you keep a positive state of mind, the illness changes to health.

The first step in healing is to heal the mind through meditation. This releases accumulated stress and prevents stress from entering the body. Through meditation, you achieve a positive state of being, health, and happiness. By practicing meditation regularly, you can bring coolness to the brain and influence the whole body-mind complex. Medical research has been exploring the connection between mind and body and linked different illnesses to our emotional condition and state of mind. When we are in emotional pain, undergo mental stress, or dealing with depression, our immunity system is negatively affected and our physical resistance to disease decreases.

Spending time in meditation reduces stress and provides physical benefits. Studies have shown that several medical conditions are positively affected by consistent reductions in anxiety. They have demonstrated improvements through meditation in diseases such as asthma, insomnia, hypertension, chronic pain, phobic anxiety, and cardiac tachyarrhythmia.

Meditation heals the mind

Life has become complicated in our times and our minds are often agitated by all kind of pressures. People have too many responsibilities and too many tasks to do in a short time. Many people hold stressful jobs that require hard work and long hours. Some even have to work two jobs in order to raise a family. For these reasons, people become off balance, irritable, and stressed-out. They may act in erratic ways and sometimes they even take out their frustration on the loved ones.

Meditation can be of great help in eliminating the lack of balance caused by stress. By spending time in meditation, we restore equilibrium to our mental functioning and create a calm. Researchers found that when we are involved in stressful situation such as driving in traffic or conflicts at work we switch in a fight or flight mode characterized by brain waves that measure from 13 to 20 Hz. In meditation, we achieve a state of deep relaxation characterized by brain waves that register between 5 and 8 Hz. The stress levels are considerably reduced in a state of deep relaxation achieved through meditation. Our mind becomes calm and calms the body in turn.

Meditation can clear emotional pollution
When you feel stressed, anxious, worried, in a bad mood, filled with negative emotions, depressed, you create emotional pollution. Your state of mind is affected by the environment and the interaction with the people around you. They either give you joy and peace, or create disturbance such as sadness, frustration, anger, or jealousy. All of these affect you when your mind is not centered

in its self. Through meditation, you can center your mind and control the emotional pollution.

Guided meditation can be an alternative therapy to heal emotional pain. You can increase your healing through meditation as you work on your emotional problems. Meditation can help as emotional therapy in several ways. First, you will see your life from a clear angle of vision, recognize the roots of your pains and solve your problems. By raising your consciousness through guided meditation, you become aware of the causes of your emotional issues and you are able to pinpoint the areas in which you need to work. Second, you contact in meditation the source of love, the spiritual energy made of the same essence as your soul. You achieve bliss, love, and higher consciousness. As you contact the divine current, you experience the divine love and connect with the love of God latent within. Contact with godly love will fill you with more love than you can ever imagine. This can heal the root cause of your emotional pain.

Through meditation's healing power, you can eliminate emotional pain.

Meditation and spirituality

Guided meditation is not only affecting your mind and body, but can also bring a spiritual transformation. You discover more about life and the mystery of the creation unfolds. You will question the meaning and purpose of life. You are very fortunate once all these questions arise in your mind. You cannot find answers for them in the books but you need to discover the answers in yourself. Living through them you will witness a transformation. You are transformed from within and achieve perfect health and wisdom.

Meditation heals the world

Guided meditation is not only transforming you but also can purify the environment. Meditation can transform violence and aggression in people to care, love, and compassion. Feelings are all around, they are not isolated in one's body. When there is a harmonious and happy feeling in a room, you'll end up feeling the same. The mind is subtler than the matter and sensitive of the energy of feelings, that are radiating throughout the place. If you feel depressed or unhappy, you are spreading it to the whole environment and you are not the only one who is feeling it..

In the current global situation of imbalances, disease, and conflicts, it's important to meditate every day. You can help to nullify the negative vibrations in the environment through meditation, and create a more harmonious environment.

The main health benefits of mediation

These are just some of the scientifically proven health benefits of guided mediation:

1. Increased immunity

Clinical studies have shown that guided meditation appears to boost immunity in recovering cancer patients and reduces the risk of cancer recurrence. When practiced daily, guided meditation boosts natural killer cells in the elderly people, giving them a greater resistance to viruses and tumors.

2. Emotional balance

Emotional balance can be achieved by freeing our mind of all the neurotic behavior that results from the existence of a traumatized ego. Guided meditation certainly is the way to cure such emotional states and unhealthy neurosis. As one's consciousness is cleansed of emotionally charged memories, great balance and freedom is achieved. As one's responses to the environment are not influenced by the emotional burdens one carries, they become instead direct, true, and appropriate.

3. Increased fertility

Clinical study have found that regular practice of mediation can increase fertility. It is proven that women are more likely to conceive when they are relaxed rather than stressed. Other studies have found that that stress reduces sperm count and motility, therefore relaxation through meditation may also boost male fertility.

4. Relieves irritable bowel syndrome

Medical research has found that patients suffering from irritable bowel syndrome can significantly improve their symptoms of constipation, diarrhea, and bloating by practicing meditation twice daily. Meditation has been proved so effective in relieving irritable bowel syndrome that it was recommended as an effective treatment by the researchers at the State University of New York.

5. Lowers blood pressure

Studies have found that meditation can lower blood pressure and make the body less responsive to stress hormones. Meditation influences blood pressure similar to blood pressure-lowering medication.

6. Anti-inflammatory

It is proved that stress leads to inflammation. Inflammation in the body tissues is a state linked to skin conditions such as psoriasis, arthritis, heart disease, and asthma. Meditation, by switching off the stress response of the body, can help prevent and treat such symptoms. Studies have shown that guided meditation clinically improved the symptoms of asthma, arthritis, and psoriasis.

7. Calmness

For the meditative mind the thoughts occur but they are just witnessed. For the ordinary mind the thoughts occur and control us. The difference between those two states of mind is that, while in both minds upsetting thoughts may occur, for those who mediate they are seen as such and are allowed to fade away. In the ordinary mind, the upsetting thoughts instigate a storm within. Meditation helps us achieve calmness and control over our thoughts and moods.

Chapter 7: Moving Deeper

Mindfulness is the practice of observation in the mind, body breath, and even the entire world. When someone practices mindfulness, they draw awareness to various aspects of their being without judgment or trying to do anything. It is the process of letting go of any regrets, guilt, or pain of the past and coming back to the moment. It also works on releasing any plans goals and working for the future. Just for a moment, this one moment, nothing else matters—not your thoughts of all those embarrassing things you did when you were younger or what you want to eat later. You come to realize that you only exist at this moment, and all your thinking does not usually help any of these things. If you sat down and wrote whatever you are thinking down, you would laugh and realize just how much garbage is floating around your brain! Such a small brain and no place to live and be; thus, we come to the practice of living and being mindful and present, finding this eternal joyfulness in this present moment of breath.

In our modern world, it seems that everything is constantly moving all the time. We run around juggling many different tasks and play many different roles. Our brains spin and spin to keep up with all this doing and offer thoughts on what to do next. Although our brain is our loyal servant directly aiding to our survival, sometimes it can feel like its all that we are. When all those things we think and wonder about pile up and become overwhelming, it is hard to find the joy and ease in our lives. Certainly, life is meant to be lived fully and enjoyed, but when our brain gets overloaded, it may become hard to make it day to day without being controlled by our minds. This is where the art of slowing down and breathing is all too necessary. To slow down and be with the breath is the best thing we can do for ourselves and our lives. Once we slow down, we realize that we live breath by breath. There is a certain closeness with life in knowing this and practicing it.

The mind has a way of getting stuck in patterns and loops that end up causing more harm than good a lot of the time. These mind patterns were formed during our evolution and were helpful for survival by reminding us we need to eat, drink water, seek shelter or safety. Brain patterns were once of service but now no longer help in the same way when it loops us around constantly towards things that we do not need to be thinking so much about. There is no use in reliving over and over the traumas of the past just as there is no need to overthink about simple things of the future. It is now time to rewire the brain and ground yourself down into being here now. All those thoughts that go on constantly in your head are unnecessary anyway, better to detach from them. When we step back and watch what the mind is doing while practicing non-attachment, we are able to see everything for simply what it is.

Labeling the things as you go is part of the practice. You can look inside your head and label the things passing through as a thought, an idea, an emotion, or maybe even a fixation. These things that occur in our heads may seem like a part of us, but in reality, they are no more than a drifting neuro pattern. When you start detaching from these things, you help yourself eliminate a lot of stress and unnecessary worry from your life. The process of detachment is meditation. Look at the things that cause you stress or some sort of emotion internally and not reacting to it. You must see it for what it is but not get caught up in any of the feelings around it. It is perfectly fine to have emotions; however, when the emotion starts to overrun and cause dysfunction in the way you live, it is time to take a step back.

This idea of mindfulness can extend itself even further out than your thoughts. You can use the practice of mindfulness to observe and label things in the body and in the breath. Observing any tensions or residual feelings in the body and letting them exist there. Or noticing how the quality of your breathing is and watching its natural course in and out of the lungs. The outside world is also a factor you can use while practicing. Watching things come and go, listening and allowing whatever it is to be there. Mindfulness practices can be used to observe and process a wide variety of subjects.

Through the practice of mindfulness, you can learn to accept things on a deeper level for what they are. By accepting all the happenings and occurrences in your thoughts, you let go of any deeper emotional attachments to them. Stress and worries will begin to not have as heavy of weight on you as before, and you will find yourself more relaxed. The practice of mindfulness meditation can greatly aid in a better night of sleep. By learning how to watch all the chaos surrounding you and just being and breathing, you will ease any stress or worries and shift yourself into a better mindset. Slowing down and being is what is required of you, and in this modern, fast-paced world, it seems like something foreign. When we are so ingrained in society to keep moving and working and resting and taking time is looked upon with laziness; It is no wonder that sitting still and breathing does not come to us as naturally as it should.

Reflect on how you exist and show up for your life every day. You may even want to do this as a journal exercise. Record the things you actually do in the day, such as waking up, stretching walking the dog, working, etc. Now think about all the reoccurring thoughts you have while going through your life—all the thoughts of doing, all the worries all the fears, and what-ifs. Now ask yourself if all these thoughts actually contribute to anything at all? Does being stressed out about money actually help your situation? Does worrying about the safety of a loved one make them any safer? No, it does not do anything for the situation. While it is a completely normal part of being a human to have these thoughts, you can ease them, so they are not giving off any harmful energy.

When you stress or worry too much, this anxious energy will follow you to bed. All this stress and anxiety will cause you to stay up late in the beta brainwaves trying to solve something you should not be trying to solve right now. Much of what keeps you up at night does not even have a solution. You are so overrun with thoughts that they seem never to take a break. To ease your insomnia, you will have to loosen the control the thoughts have over you. Luckily you can practice letting go of the power of your thoughts by learning how to be mindful.

Mindfulness meditation is not limited to only assisting sleep; it can be used at any time of day in many different types of situations. Imagine yourself stuck in traffic right now. You are sitting in a standstill on the freeway inching forward ever so slightly and slowly. It is driving you crazy, barely moving like this and you can feel the overall aggravation in the air of all the other commuters on this route. Car horns are blaring, and brake lights lie ahead for miles and miles. You are watching the clock continue with stressful thoughts of being late to work while you sit powerless and unable to change anything about the situation.

There is where a lot of aggravation and stress lie, the inability to change the situation. That is a frustrating spot to be. While we can't always be in control of our external surroundings, we can be in control of our internal environment and feelings. In times of stress and impatience when you are unable to do anything, it is best to stop and take a moment to breathe. Close your eyes or focus on a single point in this position. Feel the inhalations and exhalations of air coming through you and giving you life. Observe anything passing by in your surroundings by simply acknowledging it. Label all the things passing through your brain and label anything outside of you. It is a process of changing your inner state from agitated to relaxed. Mindfulness can help in any situation and is particularly helpful when trying to fall asleep.

Practicing mindfulness for sleep can bring you to a deeper state of ease. If you are experiencing insomnia this state of ease may have been hard to come by previously. Now that you know exactly what the root cause of your restlessness is though you can work toward changing your situation. You will do the various meditations in this book and work towards letting all the mental clutter go in this process. In the beginning, you will want to change everything, and you may find frustration when it does not change. Instead, work on accepting and allowing whatever is there to be there. Through observation without attachment, you will find this true state of meditation. Over time spent practicing, you will find it easier and easier to not only observe but let these thoughts leave you entirely. Someday you may even get to experience the wonderful feeling of not having any thoughts bother you while finding peace.

Good luck now on your journey to help your insomnia. Congratulations on taking this wonderful step toward something so beneficial and powerful. Know in your heart that you will find relief and a better state of ease and relaxation very soon. Keep up the good work practicing your meditations and allow yourself to be open and excepting. Now settle in, take a deep breath, and continue diving deeper and deeper into these practices.

Chapter 8: A Walk To The Beach At Sunrise

Relax and make yourself really comfortable. Breathe deeply, exhale and let's start our journey.

It's very early in the morning and you are going for a nice peaceful walk on a lovely peaceful beach. In the morning just before sunrise. The sunrise is far superior to the sunset as it is loaded with fresh promise and endless potential.

You are walking along an empty beach, nobody is around yet as it is so early. The sun has not even started to rise yet. You walk and walk for quite a long distance and you are beginning to unwind and relax and are feeling really good about things and yourself.

As you continue to walk further you come across some beautiful little beach huts all in a row. You walk along and can't help noticing how they all look so alike, like little boxes of candy. They are all painted in stripes, and all different colours. They look so lovely and remind you of summertime. As you walk along the row of beach huts you reach the end of the row and you gasp as you see a magnificent beach hut, it is so beautiful! It has duck egg blue clapboard exterior which brings a special rustic charm. It even has a salt-weathered veranda. Little flowers and hanging baskets are all around this charming little hut. You promptly go in to your pocket and bring out a key, and you put it in the lock and the door opens. This lovely little beach hut belongs to you. The inside is just as beautiful as the outside with its stripped floors and white washed walls. It has absolutely everything that you need inside. You decide to make yourself a well-earned cup of tea and you pull up a rocking chair and snuggle up under a blanket on the veranda.

You notice that the sun is starting to rise and a ribbon of tangerine catches your eyes. The sky has become salmon pink and you sit from your veranda and stare at this for a while. You also are aware that the tide has changed and is starting to come in. You see an expanse of wet sand just waiting for the sea to come in and take it all away.

You get up from your rocking chair and walk down to the sea. You search for a stick and start writing thoughts in to this wet sand. You write ANXIETY, DEPRESSION, WORRIES, FEAR, DOUBT. You write all the things down which are a concern to you or are causing you anxiety. You throw the stick back in to the sea and start to walk back to your beach hut.

You sit back on your rocking chair and pull the blanket around you and close your eyes for a few moments.

After a while you open your eyes after resting and you are feeling much more relaxed. You look out to the sea and notice that the sea has completely covered up all your words and they have disappeared forever. The sea and tide swept them all away.

No more worries and no more anxiety no more going over the same stuff in your head. It's all been washed away by the tide.

You now see people walking about and the little cafe and ice cream parlours are all open and ready for business. The sun is much higher in the sky now and you feel it is time to head off home. You fold up your blanket and wash your tea cup up and put your rocking chair back inside off the veranda.

You lock the door of your beach hut. You very quietly say thank you to your beach hut for allowing you to feel peace and calmness again. Your little bit of paradise!

You walk home now and get on with the rest of your day.

You are relaxed and more focused now.

SPRING TIME

Relax and make yourself very comfortable, take a few deep breaths and I shall make you feel more relaxed with this guided meditation.

Imagine yourself walking through a meadow in Spring time, when the sun is warming up and everything is starting to blossom. You are walking in to a spectacular scene. The meadow is home to a rich tapestry of wildlife.

As you continue further you find yourself walking under deciduous trees where a sea of English bluebells rekindles memories of springtime woodland walks, when the days start to lengthen and the weather starts to warm up. You are in awe of this beautiful sight.

The nodding violet blue flowers around your feet where ever you tread. These hardy native bulbs are attracting insects to their delicately scented flowers.

You are becoming very relaxed now as you walk further and further. These vigorous beauties form a dense carpet of spring colour.

You turn around from under the trees and become aware of a beautiful spring meadow. It is so beautiful that it almost takes your breath away! You decide to sit down and look across a sea of grasses swaying back and forth in the cool wind which is gently blowing through the whole meadow. You put your hand out to touch the grasses. The grasses are never static and they create a wonderful feeling of motion. Their graceful motion catches the sunlight. They make you feel wonderful and relaxed.

You stand up once more and continue to walk through the meadow being careful not to tread on the flowers. You take your shoes off and feel the earth and grass beneath your feet. You feel so free and happy that you start to skip and dance through the sea of flowers. You are light and free. You are no longer burden down with problems and worries. As you walk your way across the meadow you spot a Common Spotted Orchid, this delicate flower spreads across your meadowland in pinks and whites. You bend down and take a closer look at their beautiful blotchy leaves.

You love this feeling beneath your feet and you become aware of the Marble White butterflies with their striking black and white mosaic patterned wings. How they flutter and fly in and out of the long grasses and around your face and hair.

You hear a sound and you stop to look for it, you follow the sound and you see a Meadow Grasshopper hanging from a stork. You smile at him. This has been a fantastic experience for you today in this beautiful meadow. You sit amongst the Cowslips with their tube-like egg yolk yellow flowers all clustered together at the end of tall green stems.

You now feel quite tired after your long walk and all that dancing and skipping through the grasses, so you decide to walk back now

You walk back home feeling like your walk has taken your anxieties away and has allowed you to escape for a little while.

You can come back to the spring meadow whenever you wish to experience the beauty and sounds of the meadow,

Chapter 9: Second Week Of Meditations

As we embark on our second week of meditations, we will be dealing with slightly more advanced meditative techniques. For the first week, we used a combination of self-care and awareness meditations to help build and develop our mental strength. In the second week, you will be learning to further strengthen your mind and mental health through meditative techniques. One of the advanced meditative techniques that will be learning in this chapter includes the practice of Jhana; considered one of the most enlightened levels of Buddhist meditation.

The objective of this week is to improve your neuroplasticity by building conscious thoughts and later using that consciousness to teach your brain to react in specific patterns instead of simply observing those patterns.

8. Observing Present-Moment Meditation

The first occasion that we are dealing with today is present-moment meditation. Meditation has proven to be really important in this time period, mostly because individuals now tend to find it particularly difficult to live in the present. Because of social media and socio-cultural norms of this era, getting caught up thinking about the past or the future is commonplace, which is why individuals can often find it difficult to let go of the past or deal with future expectations. But the truth of the matter is that the experiences that you go through as a child, and as a young adult, in many ways shape who you are today. So how does one live in the present when they are constantly forced to look forward to needs that we will have at some future point, or to compensate for situations that we have faced in the past?

Well for starters you are going to want to identify them, so you can pinpoint them.These needs, both past and future, tend to take multiple forms including financial, physical and at times even mental. It is this type of strain that prevents us from acknowledging and appreciating the present moment. By identifying what needs you are required to address you can build a sense of present awareness that allows you to live more consistently in your present moment.

In order to begin this particular form of meditation it is ideal for you to first find a calm and quiet place where you can comfortably sit down and not be disturbed for the next 10 to 15 minutes. To start your present-moment meditation it is recommended that you seat yourself in an upright position. Once you have seated yourself in your position of choice, draw in a deep breath and center your focus.

You are now ready to begin your present-moment meditative journey.

Allow your eyes to slowly close, as you draw the breath into your body.

Breathe in to the count of four.

And hold.

One.

Two.

Three.

Four.
And exhale.
Repeat this exercise three additional times.
Breathe in sharply.
Hold.
One.
Two.
Three.
Four.
And exhale.
Breathe in sharply.
Hold.
One.
Two.
Three.
Four.
And exhale.
Breathe in sharply.
Hold.
One.
Two.
Three.
Four.
And exhale.
Relax.

As a strong individual it is common for you to find that, at times, it is difficult for you to focus solely on what is going on around you at that moment.

Just because something is difficult doesn't mean it can't be done.

As a strong and motivated individual you have the ability to let go of your past and focus solely on the present.

Breathe in sharply.

Hold.

One.

Two.

Three.

Four.

And exhale.

Relax.

Rememberyou are a strong and motivated person.

And as a strong and motivated person, it is important for you to be able to live in the present moment.

Breathe in sharply.

Hold.

One.

Two.

Three.
Four.
And exhale.
Relax.
The past does not concern you and the future is not something that can bend to your will. Your knowledge of this is what allows you to move forward and live your life in this moment.
Breathe in sharply.
Hold.
One.
Two.
Three.
Four.
And exhale.
Relax.
You are a part of this present moment and living in it is natural to you.
Bonus Affirmations
I will consciously choose to do better and better with each coming moment.
Today in this moment I am completely aware of the difficulties that I am faced with and regardless of them I am confident that I will persevere.

Worries, expectations and attachments are all detachable and I have chosen to detach myself from these living constraints.

I find it liberating to live in this moment. I celebrate my freedom by choosing to do what makes me happy. I am happy and fulfilled.

I am currently making a conscious choice.

My choice today is to live in a joyful and peaceful manner every moment of every day from today until the end of my days.

Today I look forward to every moment of my wonderful life. My life is wonderful because it brings with it infinite possibilities.

Today I am exactly where I was meant to be. It was suggested that I wouldn't be where I am today, and my destiny is what has brought me here.

I'm completely aware of my own consciousness. My consciousness is so strong that it allows me to control my mind in ways that were once foreign to me.

I am happy and I am worthy. I understand and accept my self-worth. I'm worth more than others believe.

Today in this moment I choose to forgive myself. It is only human error. The mistakes I have made are forgivable mistakes, from which I have learned, reflected and moved forward.

9. Entering Jhana Meditation

The next form of meditation that we will be learning is known as the entrance of Jhana. Jhana is a particular meditative experience that is commonly referred to in Sanskrit as *dhanya*. The concept of Jhana is simple. When beginners meditate, it is natural for many of their experiences allow many external distractions. Many of these distractions are often dreamlike, so much so that they form within ourselves a form of internal drama where our minds constantly in motion thinking about a wide variety of things rather than focusing on the meditative elements of your day.

Jhana is the exact opposite. Jhana allows individuals to enter state of mind where they are completely free of any external stimuli, and instead awaken to a deeper, more mindful state, where they are completely separated from worldly thoughts and worldly obstacles.

Because Jhana is such a complex form of meditation, it is always advised that it is practiced as it was originally intended to be - in an upright, full lotus position. Keep in mind that there are four levels of Jhana. Each of these levels is deeper than the previous. We will start with the first level today. Draw in a deep breath, and exhale.

You are now ready to begin your Jhana introduction.

Look around you one last time before you close your eyes and breathe in.

As you begin to fill your body with slow deep breaths, know that you are preparing yourself to enter what is known to the Buddhists as Jhana.

Breathe in carefully.

Hold.

And release.

Your mind is a gateway.

Breathe in carefully.

Hold.

And release.

Jhana is a door that leads you to a place where you can still your mind and freeze time so that there is no constant motion to distract you.

Breathe in deeply.

Hold.

And release.

As you prepare yourself to move carefully through Jhana, and as you allow your mind to enter this realm of absolute stillness, you will start to notice that the world around you has begun to slowly fade away.

Breathe in slowly.

Hold.

And release.

Today, instead of the busy distractions that are clawing for your attention, you are instead going to direct your mind to liberate itself from noise.

Breathe in slowly.

Hold.

And release.

Today your goal is simple.

You are the master of your thoughts.

Breathe in slowly.
Hold.
And release.
Your thoughts do not control you.
Breathe in slowly.
Hold.
And release.
You are in control of your thoughts.
Breathe in slowly.
Hold.
And release.
And as you remind yourself of this, you are beginning to release yourself from the constant demands you have put upon yourself.
Breathe in slowly.
Hold.
And release.
In this moment – you are free.
You are free from demands.
You are free from want.
You are free from needs of any kind.
Breathe in slowly.
Hold.
And release.
Bonus Affirmations

I am the captain of my own ship. If there is something wrong with my life, I therefore must be the one to correct it.

I am my own salvation. I do not depend on other people and I do not feel that other people need to depend on me.

I strongly believe that every morning we are born-again, and it is the choices that we make today that would impact who we will wake up as tomorrow.

Today I am motivated by love. Today love encompasses me. My life is motivated by love, and as such it is love that makes me fearless, and at the same time liberates me.

As I teach myself to fight my mind, my mind grows and rebels. I'm down teaching myself to quiet my mind, and it is with this silence that I seek for my soul to speak up.

My goal today is simple - I do not seek to control my thoughts, and I do not seek to control my mind. Today I seek only to liberate my mind from the control of my thoughts.

Today I choose to actively let go of my past. The Demons that once haunted me have been released. Instead I now dream of the future where I live for the present moment.

I see for myself a clear understanding of my own mind. To be able to understand how my mind works, and how my thoughts are processed has been my deepest wish.

Today I seek to fill my mind not with the thoughts and emotions that have constantly been running through it, but with clarity and hope.

My mind is a powerful tool. I use it to filter out negativity that the world imposes upon me. Positive thoughts lead to positive changes.

10. The Middle Stages of Jhana Meditation

Your second introduction to Jhana will bring you through the second and third stages of this particular form of meditation. Unlike the first stage of Jhana, which deals solely with the ability to think clearly and without distractions, the second stage deals with a mixture of your ability to think and your ability to critically examine. This analytical unification of your mind and consciousness is what allows you to enter the second level of Jhana. After this you face the third level. Here, once you have been able to overcome the obstacles that have been restraining you, normal human beings tend to feel a form of joy or happiness, the third Jhana teaches you how to avoid this form of heedless rapture and instead focus on serene tranquillity that in contrast, allows you to maintain a clear wakeful mindset.

Jhana should ideally be practiced in an upright full lotus position. Once again, you want to position yourself in a comfortable position, draw in a deep breath and then exhale.

You are now ready to begin your secondary Jhana meditation.

Breathe in deeply, close your eyes and begin.

In your previous meditation you learned how to enter a state of Jhana.

Breathe in slowly.

Hold.

And release.

It was here that you learned that your mind is a gateway, where you could freeze time and hold still.
Breathe in deeply.
Hold.
And release.
Jhana allows you to do more than simply sit in silence, although there is nothing that is more important than true silence.
Jhana in its most moderate form is a state of absolute clarity.
The objective of attaining jhana is to reset your mind to its most effective state.
Breathe in slowly.
Hold.
And release.
Today your goal is simple.
As the master of your thoughts, you will now use your clarified mind to analyze and see things as they are, without bias or perception.
Breathe in slowly.
Hold.
And release.
You are clear minded and unbiased.
Breathe in slowly.

Hold.
And release.
As the master of your own thoughts, you have the ability to see things for what they are instead of what you wish for them to be.
Breathe in slowly.
Hold.
And release.
And as you remind yourself of this, you present before yourself the task you wish to conduct.
Breathe in slowly.
Hold.
And release.
In this moment – you are clear minded and are thinking of the task you have been given.
You are considering the task, without bias or prejudice. And as you do a solution comes to your mind.
Breathe in slowly.
Hold.
And release.
Bonus Affirmations

The ability to think clearly supersedes one's ability to think deeply. By thinking clearly, you can enable yourself to understand the bigger picture.

The ability to think clearly is one of mankind's greatest assets. It is a weapon that that makes mankind effective, in more ways than one.

Clear thinking is enabled by clear thought. As such, it is extremely important to express yourself clearly, select those around you may understand exactly how you are processing.

Your mind is capable of all things. Its most powerful tool is the ability to think, for whatever you think, you bring to life.

What you think is what you become, and as you become a stronger person your thoughts will follow.

By teaching yourself to think positively, you're teaching yourself to envision sound as music, movement as dance, and life itself as a celebration.

Today your objective is not to hone a skill or to develop yourself, it is rather to teach yourself how to let go. The individual that you are is enough.

Today the objective is not to meditate on your thoughts but to empty your mind of them. Silence is your friend, and to enable your mind to enter a zone of silence is the best gift that you can give yourself.

The act of meditation is meant to allow your mind to shine brightly.

Meditation is what allows you to discover your own true self.

11. The Final Stage of Jhana Meditation

For the fourth level of Jhana, we will be working on the element of total and perfect self-absorption. The goal of the fourth level of Jhana is complete and utter peacefulness. Your consciousness becomes clear and balanced. There is no positivity and there is no negativity in your mind or body. The only thing that exists is a deep abiding sense of peacefulness. It is at this point that one abandons the sense of pleasure or pain, positive or negative, all for the clear absence of sensation. Stoicism is generally modeled after the fourth Jhana, and is considered to be one of the greatest philosophical branches of modern times.

It is recommended that you practice Jhana in an upright full lotus position. As you position yourself in a comfortable position, draw in a deep breath and exhale.

You are now ready to begin your final level of Jhana meditation.

Breathe in deeply, close your eyes and begin.

You have now come to explore the final stage of Jhana.

Breathe in carefully.

Hold.

And release.

After having discovered mental silence and subsequently your ability to see clearly through the fog generated in your mind, you are now moving forward once again.

Breathe in deeply.

Hold.

And release.

In the final stage of Jhana you are meant to find and attain absolute calm.

It is here that you are meant to find for yourself a divine silence that allows you to

be clear minded and peaceful in every waking moment.
Breathe in deeply.
Hold.
And release.
Serenity is commonplace for you.
Breathe in deeply.
Hold.
And release.
There is nothing around you that scares or frightens you.
Breathe in deeply.
Hold.
And release.
You are a beacon of calm, and your calm washes over you and those around you – again and again.
Breathe in deeply.
Hold.
And release.
And once again -
Breathe in carefully.
Hold.
And release.
You are clear minded and unbiased.
Breathe in carefully.

Hold.
And release.
You are calm and poised.
Breathe in carefully.
Hold.
And release.
You are at peace.
Breathe in carefully.
Hold.
And release.
There is no noise that surrounds you. You exist in perfect contentment.
Breathe in carefully.
Hold.
And release.
You are calm and poised.

Bonus Affirmations

We are what we make of our lives. The reactions we give to the changes of the universe are what determine our worth and standing.

There is nothing that is outside your reach if it is humanly possible, it is a matter of choice, not ability.

There is no reason to allow your mind to be burdened by emotions. Your mind is not a trash bin; it is not meant to store leftover feelings.

An obstacle can only continue to be an obstacle if you choose to allow it to. Difficulties are only difficulties if you see them as such. Alternatively, if you see them as an opportunity or a challenge, that is what they will present as.

Everything around you is your perception of everything around you, and by teaching yourself to distinguish fact from fiction, you are giving yourself access to a clarity of mind that is seldom found.

Your anxiety is an emotional reaction to that which you have created. You can, if you choose, throw it aside.

You have power over your mind. Your ability to control how you see or perceive things is your biggest strength.

External factors outside of your control do not deserve to be debated, thought of, or worse, pondered over.

The quickest path to happiness is to cut through the worries in your mind by distinguishing those that are within your control and those that are not.

Here the future should never disturb you. You will meet your future when you are destined to. Worrying about it will not change it, and anticipation will not make it come faster.

12. Mindful Eating Meditation

One issue that many practitioners tend to struggle with is their inability to be mindful of the way they are eating and more importantly what they are eating. Mindful meditation therefore is extremely important for individuals with troubled or complicated relationships with food, or more specifically for those who have dealt with bad eating habits, including bulimia or anorexia. Mindful eating is intended to allow practitioners to develop an awareness of exactly what they're eating in terms of the look, smell, taste and texture of the food in question, so that they can control and understand the nourishment that their body is being provided.

Mindful eating meditation is best invoked during or just before a meal and as such is generally conducted in an upright or seated position. For this form of meditation, seat yourself in front of the meal you are about to eat, and begin by first evaluating what you have on your plate before you. If you are practicing the meditation without a meal, try to start by envisioning what your typical meal looks like. As you consider the items you are about to consume, take a deep breath and exhale.

You are now ready to begin your mindful eating meditation.

Be calm and in control as you slowly begin to close your eyes in preparation for your guide.

Breathe in deeply, so that the air travels through your entire body, and then slowly allow it to release.

And again –

Breathe in.

Hold.

And release.

Food has been something that you have struggled with.

Your relationship with food stems from your inability to feel as if you are in control.

But that is about to change.

Breathe in.

Hold.

And release.

Today before you sit down with your meal, you have chosen to understand what is happening with the food that you are putting into your body.

Your body is a Temple.

You worship it by taking care of it through exercise and nourishment.

Breathe in.

Hold.

And release.

Food that you have chosen to put into your body today should help nourish your body.

If you continue to feed your body food that does not nourish, it will break and fail, like a rusty brake on a car.

Breathe in.

Hold.

And release.

The only person who has the ability to change what you are going to eat is you.
You are strong and powerful.
You are not easy to manipulate.
Advertisements cannot seduce you.
Breathe in.
Hold.
And release.
Instead you choose to be conscious and aware of what you are eating from this moment forward.

Bonus Affirmations

Today I consciously choose to be more aware of what I am eating. I'm slowing down and paying attention to the food on my plate.

My ability to eat mindfully is an extremely pleasant feeling. It allows me to be consciously aware of the people around us. It allows me to be consciously aware of the food on my plate.

I'm choosing to become mindful that my food is of a greater quality.

Today I am choosing to eat with intention.

Even though I am not able to control everything in my life, I am able to control what I put inside my body. I make conscious decisions about my food intake.

I have empowered my physical body by allowing my mind and soul to choose healthier food on a daily basis, so that I have a more nutritious diet.

The food that I am putting inside my body is the medicine that I'm giving my body.

I'm keeping my body healthy, so that it does not require chemicals to stabilize itself.

There is a voice in my mind that is my internal nutritionist. My foot needed has allowed me to become reacquainted with this voice.

Food is not the enemy. I enjoy consciously being able to choose what food I am going to eat, preparing my meal, and consciously keeping myself in sync with my food.

I choose to eat for the sake of eating. Every additional spoonful food, in any form, that I put on my plate is there so that I can use it to energize my body. I need energy so that I can commit to doing new things and good things. Food is my body's fuel, as I give my body just enough so as not to overflow the tank.

13. Mindful Observation Meditation

The next form of meditation that you will be learning is known as the mindful observation technique. This type of mindfulness is a skill that allows individuals to consciously begin to notice what is happening in the present moment, and focus on that. Similar to the present moment meditation which encourages individuals to focus on a specific moment in time, mindful observation techniques also allow individuals to use their observation skills check in with what is going on in their lives during this time of their life. The ability to detach from past and future constraints allows individuals to make better informed decisions about what is best for them.

In order to begin your mindful observation meditation, first find a quiet place where you will not be bothered for at least 10 to 30 minutes. Keep in mind that observational mindfulness is also best done in a seated position. You can also explore using kneeling or lotus positions, if you feel more comfortable.

Once you have seated yourself appropriately, begin the meditation by drawing in a deep breath and centering your focus.

You are now ready to begin your mindful observation meditation.

Breathe in deeply, and begin.

You are constantly surrounded by different needs and demands that you are expected to meet.

Various needs and demands that you were expected to meet cause you to feel an immense burden. Because of this, you find it difficult to observe your surroundings.

Breathe in.

Hold.

And release.

And again, breathe in.

Hold.

And release.

As you feel the breath enter your body, remind yourself that you are capable of being a calm, mindful individual.

Your ability to be mindful is what has allowed you to conquer anxiety and move fearlessly towards the future, by living in the present.
Breathe in.
Hold.
And release.
The objective of mindfulness is not to help you know and remember, but instead it is meant to allow you to identify how you feel.
Breathe in.
Hold.
And release.
As you observe the world around, you will notice that certain emotions come to you when you are faced with certain tasks.
You are not meant to be controlled by these emotions, you are meant simply to observe them and to understand them.
Breathe in.
Hold.
And release.
Your ability to be mindful teaches you to be strong and silent. The ability to

respond does not mean that you must respond.

Breathe in.

Hold.

And release.

You are mindful. You are learning to be more mindful everyday.

Breathe in.

Hold.

And release.

Mindfulness helps you move forward in life.

Bonus Affirmations

Mindfulness is simple. The only task you need to keep in mind is that of being mindful.

The easiest way to conquer anxiety, is to stop worrying about the past, or living in fear of the future. Allow yourself instead to live in the present moment. It's here that you will find solitude and peace.

By allowing yourself to sit in silence, with the wind blowing through your hair, and thoughts swirling through your mind, you realize that you are one with the universe.

By allowing yourself to surrender is to you allow yourself to grow into whoever it is you were meant to be.

Impulsiveness is the opposite of mindfulness. Where mindfulness teaches yourself to let go, impulsiveness teaches you to move forward, without testing the waters.

Once you're able to identify how you feel, you'll find it much easier to deal with emotion.

Mindfulness teaches you to not react to things, and instead to respond to them.

The best lesson of mindfulness deals with teaching individuals to live in the actual moment. Life is about the now.

Wherever you are, whenever you are, allow yourself to be there in that moment, completely.

Mindfulness is there to help you remember, not tangible things or abstract moments, but clarity and silence.

14. Emotional Control Meditation

A common problem that most individuals face is that they find it hard to control their emotions or their feelings. When faced with certain situations it is natural for your emotions to sometimes hold you hostage. But what is natural is not necessarily good for you. On the contrary, it is important for you to consciously choose to feel a sense of calm serenity in order to have a more grounded and healthier lifestyle. The best way to dissolve the sense of intense emotional constraint is to train yourself to be emotionally resilient. The more you learn to control the extreme highs and lows of your emotions regardless of the trigger, the stronger and more resilient you become mentally. Keep in mind the average emotional life cycle is only about 90 seconds. That however doesn't mean that emotions don't exist for longer than one and a half minutes. It simply means that if you are trapped in an emotion for longer than that, then odds are that you may be dealing with a retained emotion that you have not yet had an opportunity to deal with or address.

Fortunately, with the following meditation, you will finally have an opportunity to practice controlling your thoughts and emotions, and keeping them positive. Start by finding a calm, quiet place where you can begin. Once you find a comfortable posture, draw in a deep breath and exhale.

You are now ready to begin your emotional control meditation.

Breathe deeply in, and as you do, allow your eyes to close, slowly.

Today your meditative guide will center around your ability to mentally control your emotions.

Start by holding your breath for four seconds and count down as you breathe out.

One.

Two.

Three.

Four.

Now, consciously allow your back to relax, bringing yourself into the present moment.

Consciously relax your shoulders and then your neck. You will find that, at a point,

you can start to feel the world around you vibrate with the energy you are releasing.
Ask yourself, what energy is it that you are releasing today?
How do you feel?
Breathe in gently.
Hold.
One.
Two.
Three.
Four.
And release.
Feel the present surround you.
And ask yourself again – how do you feel?
As you start to categorize your feelings, ask yourself why you feel the way you feel today.
Breathe in gently.
Hold.
One.
Two.
Three.
Four.
And release.
Try to consciously identify your emotional trigger points.

As you begin to list them, try to then identify if you have acted in any specific manner due to the emotional triggers you have faced.

Breathe in gently.

Hold.

One.

Two.

Three.

Four.

And release.

You are a strong independent individual.

You are capable of consciously choosing to acknowledge your emotions without allowing your emotions to take control of you.

Breathe in gently.

Hold.

One.

Two.

Three.

Four.

And release.

Understand, that in this moment, you are in control.

There is nothing that can take control away from you.
There is nothing that can force you to do anything you don't want.
Breathe in gently.
Hold.
One.
Two.
Three.
Four.
And release.
At this very moment, calmly try to visualize the emotions that you have been feeling throughout your body the entire day.
Breathe in gently.
Hold.
One.
Two.
Three.
Four.
And release.
As you visualise this emotion, imagine yourself tying a tight leash around its neck and reigning it back in.
Breathe in gently.

Hold.
One.
Two.
Three.
Four.
And release.
Remember in this moment you are in control.
There is nothing that can take control from you.
There is nothing that can force you to do anything you don't want.
Breathe in gently.
Hold.
One.
Two.
Three.
Four.
And release.
Bonus Affirmations
I consciously choose to acknowledge all of my emotions. The only emotion that I will retain within myself are ideas that allow me to elevate my true identity.

Every day I am becoming more and more aware of the impact of my emotions on my successes and my failures.

I consciously choose to control my emotions. In this moment, I am replacing anger with understanding, and fear with love.

I take control of my emotions by changing my thoughts. Today I am practicing feeling positive and positivity is a part of my daily life.

I make it a point to honor my feelings. My feelings tell me things about myself that I don't necessarily understand.

I'm practicing control. Today I'm practicing finding a way to ensure that I have complete control over my inner images, my visualizations, and my dialogues.

I am calm level headed individual. I'm calm in all circumstances. I do not allow external pressures to scare me or force my hand.

I believe that my feelings are empowering me to be a better person each and every day.

Negative emotions tell me that I'm doing something that is not in my own best interest. My positive emotions shelter me and show me where I need to be going.

The feelings that I indulge in are important. I consciously choose to ensure that the feelings that I allow inside my own mind are good positive images that allow me clarity of thought.

Chapter 10: Exploring The Practice Of Meditation

You don't need anything else to meditate except an open mind, but here are some tips which can encourage exercise. When you find yourself frustrated or depressed about your work, go back to this section. Meditation is to everybody. In yoga, we often hear people say, "Oh, I can't do yoga; I'm not flexible at all." This excuse baffles me because it means people assume that what's a result of the practice (flexibility) is a prerequisite for even trying it, which is simply not true. To meditation, a similar concept applies. If you're someone who thrives on business and describes yourself as nervous, tired, or stressed out, then you may find meditation isn't for you. Trying meditation would be such a smart idea for you. Meditation will help people in their minds and lives find space and peace. This also shows that your self-concepts ("I'm too busy") are just feelings—so you don't have to believe them anymore.

You've got the Time. Just some brief minutes of meditation is better than zero. I know it can be hard to prioritize anything that appears not "productive" at first. Still, the reality is that meditation is incredibly productive, maybe one of the most productive things you can do with 5 or 10 minutes. Take your time. You just don't need a number. Try to put your next practice on the calendar or set the alarm on your phone. Commit and follow through—I know that somewhere in your day, you can find 5 to 10 minutes...

CREATING THE SPACE

You can meditate anywhere—on the train, in a plane, in a conference room, in a hotel lobby. Trying to lower distractions can be helpful, particularly in the beginning. You don't need a special cushion or chair, but you want to be comfortable physically. More noise makes concentrating at first easier, so find the quietest spot possible. You can also listen on the headphones or speakers to calming ambient music to block out any background noise. Find a place at home where you can have some privacy and warmth, and make that place your dedicated spot for meditation.

UNPLUGGING

Put your phone in airplane mode (unless you need it for music with headphones, in which case all alerts should be switched off). Turn the computer off or put it in sleep mode. Switch off any alarms, which could disturb you. The present moment often involves obstacles beyond our control, which can be daunting but which are necessary to embrace. Our digital lives are one area beyond our influence, so unplug and put electronics away before you settle in.

GETTING RELAXED

Try to find a comfortable spot wherever you are. You may sit on a chair, a bench, or a seat on the floor. Seek to find a place where after a few minutes, you won't get tired and where your legs won't fall asleep. When you're in a public location, position yourself to prevent distractions, so that you're not in the way. For some reason, if sitting is not going to work for you, lying flat on your back can work, but you run the risk of falling asleep. Ideally, you're going to want to be relaxed but not so comfortable you're going to doze off.

All you've got to do is try. Remember this advice as you begin your practice: meditation cannot "fail." Yes, you may be struggling with it, but you do have seasoned practitioners struggling. Go on yourself smoothly. There are no meditation rules, so don't be too rigid about it. Even meditation can be worth 30 seconds. Only carve out the time every practice calls for and try to focus your mind on the present moment. With time, you'll find a rhythm and a method that works for you. You'll enjoy the benefits of meditation so long as you try.

How Do I Know If Meditation Works?

Remember that meditation is intended to cultivate a clear awareness of the present moment. When you do so, you will begin to see your feelings as opinions, not as realities, and you will begin to find space between stressors and your responses.

Through these practices, there is an infinite number of ways your practice of meditation will help you in your life. Whether you begin to note that you're taking deeper breaths all day long, or that you're letting thoughts go rather than capturing them, or that you're just more comfortable, happy or getting better sleep, you'll know that meditation works.

HOW TO MAKE THIS BOOK WORK FOR YOU

This book is your journal, built to help you practice meditation. Practices in meditation are separate from each other, and you don't need to do them in any specific order. Choose the activities that you like best and replicate as much as you like. And begin by trying out a new meditation for each practice before you settle in on an approach that works best for you. Consider the meditations that follow as the first steps down a fascinating, open-ended road of self-discovery. These are designed primarily to reduce stress, promote relaxation, and enhance the quality of your sleep, but you can encounter still more pronounced changes. Don't let them run away. Continue along the way. Keep on exploring.

Stretch Out Yourself and the Practice

The book cover varies in length—some are 5 minutes, others are 25 minutes. I encourage all of you to try them out. By simply reading them, you will not be able to know which ones work best for you. You got to do them. Start with the shorter practices and get up to work. As you become more comfortable, try the methods longer and longer.

Admit Your Frustration

With your practice, you'll almost definitely feel some irritation or restlessness from time to time (maybe even every time). Remember that feelings are your mind's creations. Wait them out, and let them go. If they're so strong, you find it impossible to get back into your meditation, then step away is okay. Don't let that time be the last time you've ever attempted meditation, and don't keep any anger feelings on. Let them go, regroup, do something else, revisit the values here, and start again. Also, the most experienced meditators still encounter strong psychological and emotional resistance, as I described earlier. That kind of strength is usual. You can only accept it for what it is.

Let the Journey Continue

I genuinely believe in the influence of meditation, as is no longer evident by now. I am delighted to share with you the following activities, and I genuinely hope you will consider them helpful. When you're new to meditation, often refer to this chapter for encouragement and a reminder you're on the right track. Remember that you are embarking on a journey during which you may encounter new experiences and rediscover yourself, so seeking more room, clarity, relaxation, so rest is the ideal outcome. Worth taking this trip.

Chapter 11: Relaxation And Stress Scripts

Now that you are completely relaxed, I want you to take note of how you are feeling as a whole. How are you doing at this moment? How does your body feel?

Take a few moments and scan your body. There is no need to judge yourself right now. All I want you to do is notice is how your body is feeling from your head to your toes.

Scan through your body from your feet...to your ankles...all the way up your legs...and into your hips. At your own pace, scan your body through your stomach, chest, hands, shoulders, neck, head, and face.

We worked on relaxing before to help deepen into your practice, but you may notice certain areas where you are still tense. You have noted where you are stressed. Now, gently take note of where your body is most relaxed.

As you focus on your body, notice how it begins to relax with no conscious effort. As you scan your body, feel as the muscles become looser and less tense on their own. All you need to do is lay quiet and remain relaxed. You feel happy that this is happening naturally. With each passing moment, your body falls more relaxed, even more, ready to fall asleep.

Now that you are feeling more relaxed, I want to talk about your body image. Many of us move through the day, uncomfortable, simply because we are not happy with our self and the way we look. But what is body image? Are you thinking about what your body looks like? Perhaps you are thinking about the ideas you have about your body. How are you feeling about your physical self at this moment? What does body image mean to you?

Inhale...and exhale...

As you continue to focus on your breath, I invite you to take a few moments to consider the thoughts and ideas you have about your body. How do these thoughts make you feel as you scan over your own body image? For some, you may feel comfortable and content. For others, you are unhappy, unaccepting, or dissatisfied. Perhaps, there is a combination depending on how kind you are to yourself. However, you feel, accept the emotions you are feeling at this moment.

Stay with me for a moment. I invite you to ponder how it would feel to accept your body the way it is? How would it feel to be okay with your physical self? Take a few moments now to breathe, and picture in detail how this would feel.

Breathe in...and breathe out...wonderful.

Now, try to think of a moment in your life when you accepted your physical self. Whether it be your whole self or a part of your self that you really enjoy, think of a moment.

Which part of your body do you accept?

Imagine now, how it would feel to accept your whole body as opposed to thinking of yourself as a collection of separate parts. If you are beginning to feel stressed out over these thoughts, allow us to take a few steps back to return to relaxation.

Notice certain parts tensing up at this moment. Make a note of these locations and focus positive energy to return these body parts to total relaxation. Inhale...and exhale...you are safe and loved at this moment. You are calm and relaxed...inhale...and exhale...

When you have returned to a state of total relaxation and calmness, I invite you to repeat the following body image affirmations after me. If you don't feel like repeating these, try to listen and relax as I speak. As you work on a positive body image, you may feel yourself less stressed through the day. When we love ourselves, it grants us the ability to spread that love to others. Perhaps if you loved yourself more, you would take the time to release stress and enjoy a peaceful night's rest. Who knows, perhaps your body image has been bringing you down more than you ever imagined.

When you are ready, repeat after me. Each affirmation I am about to say is completely true. Even if you don't believe it, you will work through your negative thoughts until you believe them to be so. Let's begin.

I am perfect the way I am.
(Pause)
I choose to accept the way I am.
(Pause)
My body is acceptable the way it is at this moment.
(Pause)
I choose to accept the body I am in.
(Pause)
I am a wonderful person as a whole.
(Pause)
There is no reason to be perfect.
(Pause)
I have imperfections, and that is okay.
(Pause)
I love the person that I am.
(Pause)
I am human, and I have flaws.
(Pause)
I choose to accept these flaws.
(Pause)
I will stop judging my body.
(Pause)
I am in love with who I am.
(Pause)
I choose to accept myself.

(Pause)

I love myself so that I can love others.

Wonderful. Feel free to repeat these affirmations as often as you need. Now that we have gone through some, how are you feeling? Whatever you are feeling at this moment is perfectly acceptable. Perhaps you believe every word I have told you, and perhaps you don't. As you practice positive body image more, you may find yourself becoming less stressed and much happier.

Take a few moments now to return to relaxing. Any tension or stress you may have after thinking about your body can be let go with each breath you take. Remember what I taught you about deep breathing. I want you to continue to breathe deep and natural. Ready?

Inhale…and two…and three…and four…and pause…two…three…and exhale…two…three…four…five…

Inhale…and two…and three…and four…and pause…two…three…and exhale…two…three…four…five…

Inhale...and two...and three...and four...and pause...two...three...and exhale...two...three...four...five...

Inhale...and two...and three...and four...and pause...two...three...and exhale...two...three...four...five...

Inhale...and two...and three...and four...and pause...two...three...and exhale...two...three...four...five...

You are doing a wonderful job. Now that we have gone over the emotions of your body image, I would like to go over a progressive muscle relaxation exercise to help your body heal itself. This is a vital exercise to help you get the most out of the sleep you are soon to slip into. When your body is relaxed and comfortable, you will sleep deeper and wake up feeling more refreshed.

As you continue to focus on your breath, I invite you first to release the tension from the bottom of your feet. Imagine how it would feel to step into a nice, warm bathtub. How does this sensation feel to you? Does the warm water tingle? Feel as your feet fall loose and imagine this feeling of total relaxation washing from your feet and up into your ankles.

This sensation rises gently over your ankles and flows up your lower legs until it begins to kiss your knees gently. At this point, you allow the sensation of relaxation spread through your whole body. It rises around your hips and through your pelvic areas.

You gently give into the sensation as it washes over your stomach, hugs around your lower back and continues to rise over your chest. As this happens, relax your upper arms, lower arms, and wrist. The sensation flows over the palms of your hands. Imagine the sensation flowing to each finger. Your hands feel pleasant, relaxed, and warm.

Bring your focus back to your breath, and the relaxation spreads through your collar bones, across your shoulders and washes down your entire back again. Sink into the bed further and take a deep, cleansing breath in…and let it go slowly.

Now, allow the sensation up even further as it spreads across your chin, through your mouth, your cheeks, it gently caresses your nose and up to your eyes. At this point, your eyelids feel peaceful and heavy with relaxation.

Allow the relaxation to wash over the top of your head. Feel your eyebrows relaxing. Your forehead is smooth and cool. The relaxation has washed over your whole body, and you can feel it flowing from your head to your feet.

You are completely relaxed now. Feel as this sensation flows down your spine. It starts at the top, down your neck, into your upper back...middle back...lower back...and gently makes it way down your tailbone in the very bottom of your spine. Feel as every muscle relaxes around your spine. Breathing is coming so easily and naturally for you; you aren't even thinking about it.

As you continue to breathe, complete another body scan. Are there any areas of tension left? If so, direct the flow of relaxation into that area. This energy has the ability to lift and carry the tension away. Imagine the air you are breathing as the energy to cleanse your body. Each time you breathe in, picture the tension leaving your body every time you breathe out.

When you are ready, I want you to create an image in your head. I want you to picture your current state of being. Are there any physical ailments that have been bothering you? Perhaps you have an injury, an illness, or just overall pain you have been dealing with. It does not matter if this is something that has been diagnosed just yet. Whatever the problem is, imagine this problem in your mind, and we will work on healing it through this guided meditation.

With this specific location in mind, I want you to picture this area being dark. Truly picture this area in detail. What does it look like? How does it feel? Create a clear mental image in your mind, and we will begin.

Now, picture healing relaxation as light. Imagine this light flowing through your whole body, and then direct the light toward the dark area. When we put forth the effort, our body has a wonderful way of healing itself.

This healing light has the ability to promote strength, it can support your immune system, and promotes the growth of healthy tissue in our body. This healing light can also clean your body and help you to remove any waste, bacteria, or toxins that are hanging out in you. It also has the ability to remove any unhealthy matter from your body so that you can be the healthiest version of yourself.

As you picture the light moving through you, imagine that it begins to swirl and focus on the dark area. Notice how small pieces of this area begin to be carried away by the light. Notice this and allow the dark pieces to leave your body. Gently breathe in the healing energy and breathe out any tension or illness you have been holding onto.

You have the power to allow this light to heal the problem areas you have in your body. Imagine the dark area in your body become completely enveloped by the healing light. Slowly, the dark area becomes lighter and lighter. Your immune system is working hard to heal you, and the light travels to any area you truly need it in.

Now, the healing light courses through your whole body. It fills you with complete health and relaxation. Any problem areas in your body, the light seeks and makes healthy again. It is carrying away your discomfort and healing you to the best version of yourself.

Allow this to happen. Continue to take cleansing breaths in and breathe out any negative matter you have been holding onto.

Breathe in total relaxation…and breathe out the old…

Now, I invite you to take a few moments to relax and enjoy this healing process. Feel as your confidence begins to grow now that you have worked on improving your body image and healing your body. You feel as your body grows more relaxed and readier to fall into a restful night's sleep. You feel wonderful, happy, and completely stress-free.

You are doing wonderfully. In a few moments, we will be moving onto exercises so you can fall asleep. Before we get there, I want you to turn your focus inward. Take a deep, truthful look inside to find your authentic self.

As you do this, begin to reflect on your values. What is important to you? What do you value most in life? Why is it that you chose this audio to help release stress so that you can sleep better at night? For the next few moments, I invite you to focus on your breath and ask yourself these very important questions.

(Pause)

Breathe in...breathe out...

These values you have been thinking about are a major part of what makes you who you are. If you are being true to your core values, these beliefs are what drive your behavior. When you live true to your values, you will be much happier.

I now invite you to think of your values and think how you can incorporate them into your day-to-day life. When you are ready, I want you to now think of what else makes you the person that you are.

When we find out authentic self, this gives us the ability to learn who we really are. Our authentic selves are the person we are meant to be. When we try to be who we are not, this can hold you back and create a lot of stress.

If you are telling yourself that you are not being your authentic self, I want you to imagine the type of person you want to be. Take a deep breath and imagine observing yourself. How are you acting? Is this the person you are or who you want to be?

Now, I want you to picture yourself standing in an empty room. Imagine that you are stripping away everything that is holding you back from your true potential. Your self-doubt begins to dissolve, and, in its place, confidence takes over. This person you are picturing lets go of anything that stands between you and success. You let go of illness, baggage from the past, and lack of resources. When you are your authentic self, there is nothing to stand in between you and your goals. Watch as all of these problems disappear and go away for good.

What is left when you strip all of these problems away? This person is who you are at the core. All of your character traits and personality makes you who you are, and that is all you can ask of yourself. You work hard. You are a committed person. You are in love with your life.

We all have issues to work through, what is important is that you work on them every day. There is always room for improvement, and that is why you are here. You are letting go of the stress, finding yourself, and learning how to become the best version of yourself.

With all of these positive changes you have made in just one night, it is time to put your mind to rest. You have done a wonderful job of working on your well-being. At this moment, you are feeling calm and relaxed. You have let go of your worries, explored your true self, and found your authentic core. When you are ready, take a deep breath in and let it go.

At this moment, you should feel completely calm and at peace. Your body begins to gently tell you that it is time to fall asleep. In the next few moments, we will begin to place your mind and soul at rest. You will sleep peacefully and deep through the night. In the morning, you will awaken feeling calm and well rested at the time you need to wake up.

When you fall asleep, you will automatically fall out of your trance. Your subconscious will do all of the work for you. All you need to do right now is focus on your breath and allow yourself to fall asleep for the night.

Chapter 12: Breathing Meditation

Easy Breathing Meditation to Improve Mindfulness, Diaphragm Meditation for Panic Disorders, Relaxing the Body, Targeted Muscle Group Relaxation Script, Relaxation, and Physical Hypnosis Meditation

There is a wide scope of ways that reflection alone can help. Regardless, breathing thought has many unique points of interest that can improve your cerebrum and body. While it likely will not seem much, breathing reflection can be mind-blowing when realized properly. In this chapter, we will discuss a segment of the key points of interest that breathing consideration can have on your general prosperity.

Improved Ability to Focus

Another noteworthy advantage that can come from fusing breathing activities into your everyday life would be a superior capacity to unwind. Breathing activities have appeared to assist one's capacity with experiencing dreary musings and feelings without encountering passionate trouble because of them.

Subsequently, this sort of breathing can truly help those lessen the negative passionate swings that normally accompany redundant musings and stressing. This by itself will take into account one to be better ready to loosen up when consolidating this sort of breathing contemplation into one's day by day schedule. Alongside this, it has been demonstrated that breathing activities like profound breathing can have an enormously positive effect on decreasing feelings of anxiety. Having decreased feelings of anxiety is probably going to prompt having a greatly improved capacity to unwind and to diminish the nervousness that regularly originates from monotonous musings. Profound breathing has additionally demonstrated a characteristic capacity to help lower circulatory strain and decrease cortisol reaction.

Improved Ability to Relax

Another critical advantage that can originate from joining breathing activities into your day-by-day life would be a superior capacity to unwind. Breathing activities have appeared to assist one's capacity with experiencing redundant considerations and feelings without encountering passionate misery as a result of them.

Thus, this sort of breathing can truly help those diminish the negative enthusiastic swings that regularly accompany tedious considerations and stressing. This by itself will consider one to be better ready to loosen up when consolidating this kind of breathing contemplation into one's day-by-day schedule. Alongside this, it has been demonstrated that breathing activities like profound breathing can have a colossally positive effect on lessening feelings of anxiety. Having diminished feelings of anxiety is probably going to prompt having a greatly improved capacity to unwind and to lessen the uneasiness that commonly originates from dreary contemplations. Profound breathing has additionally demonstrated a characteristic capacity to help lower pulse and diminish cortisol reaction.

Enhanced Self-Awareness

Another advantage that can emerge out of fusing breathing meditation in one's day-by-day life is simply the capacity to improve one's mindfulness. In all honesty, however, saving time for this sort of contemplation will enable one to self-reflect. This will enable one to truly deal with and see how your mind and body respond to specific circumstances and that is only the tip of the iceberg. This is principal because breathing reflection necessitates that you center around breathing and it enables you to deliberately perceive how your contemplations meander and how your body responds to them.

Improved Self-Control

Another beneficial thing that can emerge out of breathing activities is simply the capacity to improve one's control. Many individuals frequently respond in a split second. When you consolidate breathing activities and contemplation in your life, you will almost certainly better figure out how to manage one's passionate reactions. This by itself is going to make one a substantially more patient individual largely and enable one to have the option to more readily deal with the passionate reactions that accompany different activities.

Breathing thoughts enable you to figure out how to control your feelings on the cognizant level and it can decidedly reflect in your capacity to keep up discretion in even the hardest situations. It can enable one to accomplish a specific degree of care that can streamline poise such that very few different practices can. Studies have demonstrated that it tends to be viable and snappy for those that have exhibited a failure to control themselves for different reasons. This incorporates those that may experience the ill effects of dependence because of an absence of discretion or even those that may be not able to stick with a solid way of life changes.

Better Emotional Health

Another advantage that can come legitimately from breathing thoughts would be better enthusiastic wellbeing. As referenced beforehand, breathing and care, thoughts have appeared to viably limit misery musings in those that experience them.

This is fundamental because of the capacity to emphatically affect the negative reactions that monotonous musings can have on one's passionate state. Those that cannot control or deal with the passionate reactions that accompany these considerations commonly reach or enter a condition of discouragement. By fusing breathing reflection in one's life, it should help break the negative reactions that can happen from these dull considerations and enable one to be better ready to manage them in a positive way. Therefore, it stays probably the ideal approaches to normally ward off side effects of both misery and nervousness.

Breathing Meditation Exercises to Improve Mindfulness

Breathing is the way to accomplishing care. It's basically why you feel altogether more stunning doing yoga than you do during high impact exercise; you're controlling your breathing while at the same time getting yourself every one of the advantages that pursue a quiet, constant flow of outside air.

In any case, not all breathing is made similarly. You likely took in this in your yoga classes. You need to show yourself how to inhale appropriately so as to boost the advantages, and there are a few breathing methods you can use, specifically, while meditating.

Here is a portion of the preferred breathing methods we like to utilize when meditating with our mala dabs.

The Common Yoga Breathing Technique

In the event that you do yoga on a daily level, you likely definitely know this system as its most usually utilized all through various styles of yoga. It is frequently used to quiet your breathing, so you can savor the advantages of new oxygen. To do this breathing procedure, pursue these means:

1. Take a moderate, full breath in
2. Pause
3. Slowly let your breath out

Equal Breathing

A breathing system that is sure to help quiet the mind, body, and soul is called equal breathing. It is ideal for decreasing pressure, quieting your nerves and expanding the center, and should be possible anywhere and whenever. Here are the means for this breathing method:

1. Take a moderate breath in through your nose for a tally of four
2. Slowly breathe out through your mouth for a tally of four

Count of Four

A typical breathing procedure for contemplation is to just check to four, at that point tally in reverse from four, all coordinated with your breath. You can likewise utilize various numbers, contingent upon your inclinations however as you will find in this post, a check of four

is by all accounts the shared factor. Here are the means:
1. Breath in – count to one
2. Breath out – count to two
3. Breath in – count to three
4. Breath out – count to four
5. Breath in – count to three
6. Breath out – count to two
7. Breath in – count to one
8. Breath out – count to two
9. Repeat

Abdominal Breathing

Stomach breathing is one of the most prompt breathing methodologies, so it is dependably bolstered for understudies starting to consider. Regardless, it works for everyone, can be used in, and outside of your mind, as it is a stunning framework to diminish stress at some optional time. It nearly just takes a couple of minutes to do, making it perfect for a condition where you need to study yourself:

Place a hand on the chest

Place another hand on your abdomen

Now take a breath with your nose

Feel as your hand on top of your stomach moves up and down as you breathe with your stomach

Now slowly release your breath

The Stimulating Breath

The Stimulating Breath is additionally called the Cries Breath and it is incredible for expanding sharpness and vitality. It can take some training to consummate yet once you do, you will feel animated and will move toward becoming finished dependent on the manner in which it makes you feel. Here are the means:

1. Quickly breathe in and breathe out through your nose, as short as could reasonably be expected, guaranteeing the length is equivalent for both
2. Aim to get three breathes in and breathes out every second
3. Continue for five seconds
4. Slowly increment your time all through your training until you arrive at one entire moment

Alternate Nostril Breathing

Another basic breathing procedure utilized during contemplation and yoga is the other nostril breathing – and truly, it is actually, what it seems like. Doing this strategy permits you to reenergize your psyche, body, and soul. Here are the means:

1. Plug your right nostril with your right thumb
2. Take a full breath through the left nostril
3. Remove your thumb from your right nostril and fitting your left nostril with your ring finger
4. Slowly breathe out
5. Repeat

The 4-7-8 Count

The 4-7-8 count, generally rang the slackening breath technique, is one of the most direct to do and as a touch of a bonus, the points of interest are exponential. This movement can quickly calm the tangible framework, to such a degree, that it can feel like your nerves have been quieted. Hence, it is surprising for anyone wanting to calm their mind or who encounters anxiety or rest a dozing issue. Here is the way by which you do it:

1. Rest the tip of your tongue at the top back of your teeth
2. Let out a significant breath out, close by a noteworthy groan or whooshing sound
3. Close your mouth and bit by bit take in through your sense about a count of four
4. Hold your breath for a check of seven
5. Exhale significantly and absolutely for a check of eight, being sure to let out a noteworthy groan or whooshing sound
6. Repeat

Skull Shining Breath

This breathing strategy, otherwise called Kapalabhati, is an extraordinary method to shake off negative vitality and warm up your psyche, body, and soul. It tends to be utilized in the first part of the day, preceding a test, before your next yoga class or during contemplation. Here is the way to do it:

1. Take a long, slow breath in
2. Quickly let out an incredible breathe out from your stomach out
3. Repeat

Mala Bead Breathing

On the off chance that checking is not your thing or you are basically too overpowered, occupied or worried to keep tally, mala beads are the ideal arrangement. Customarily, these contemplation gadgets were utilized to follow your breath, but with no checking. You essentially move your fingers along the mala beads, one for every breath. The key is to pick the privilege mala bead for your aim, as the vitality from the common stone can advance your contemplation and unwinding. Here are the means:

1. Choose a mala bead explicit to your aim (explanation behind doing the breathing strategy)
2. Hold the mala bead in your correct hand
3. Drape it between your center and forefinger
4. Starting at the master bead, move your thumb along each littler bead, taking in for each
5. Do this on numerous occasions, until you are back at your primary bead. Breathing is the least demanding, most moderate and inarguably, the most dominant type of

treatment. In this way, pick a breathing strategy and some mala beads that suit your needs, and receive the rewards of legitimate relaxing.

Diaphragm Meditation for Panic Disorders

Unwinding systems are procedures used to help with overseeing alarm indications, diminishing pressure, and inspiring a feeling of quiet. Such methods can likewise be used to help in mitigating extraordinary nervousness and traversing fits of anxiety. The accompanying portrays the unwinding strategy of profound breathing (otherwise called stomach breathing). Begin rehearsing this procedure today to start feeling increasingly loose.

Profound breathing is additionally regularly the establishment for some other unwinding procedures, for example, primary muscle relaxation (PMR), reflection, and representation.

Your breathing assumes a significant job in dealing with the side effects of frenzy issue. In spite of the fact that you may not be aware of your breathing procedure, almost certainly, your breathing winds up quickened while having apprehensive or anxious feelings.

Breathing with your chest does not take into consideration full, total breaths are regularly connected with expanded sentiments of tension. Truth be told, one of the most well-known indications for fits of anxiety is hyperventilation or brevity of breath.

When full breaths are taken more they enable a sense of quiet to come and allow you to remain in charge although you may feel uneasy or frenzy. Activities for breathing can allow you to adapt to the brevity of breath, alongside other normal uneasiness and frenzy related indications, for example, diminishing quickened pulse and alleviating muscle pressure.

Relaxing the body

When stressors are faced throughout every day, we are able to convey mental and physical pressures because of them being able to benefit from each other. Feeling physically tense can expand your mental and enthusiastic pressure and the other way around. On the other hand, loosening up your body physically can help alleviate mental pressure, and loosening up your brain can push you to physically unwind and discharge strain in your body. At the point when your pressure reaction is never again activated, it ends up far simpler to approach difficulties in a proactive, tranquil manner.

Figuring out how to ace methods that empower the two sorts of unwinding is a profoundly successful course to push help.

The most effective method to Loosen up Your Psyche and Body

On the off chance that you are feeling centered and contemplating how to loosen up, here are some simple steps for releasing weight in your physical make-up and your brain.

Comprehend That You Need to Loosen up

Various people genuinely endeavor past their stress by means of neglecting it and believing the stressors go by quickly, although stressors can be created. Along these lines, it is normal to be found napping by pressure when you arrive at the purpose of inclination overpowered or to be worried to the point that it is incurring significant damage without understanding that you have to deal with dealing with a portion of the worry in your life and your mind.

It is basic to know about when you have an extreme amount of pressure and need to loosen up.

Loosen up Physically

Physically slackening up your body would instantly be able to help with weight since it thwarts and turns around your pressure response and can end a negative-analysis cycle where your mind responds to fear by hailing a substantial strain response. The worry in your body that can final product from this response assembles the scopes of stress you experience deep down. There are various positive strategies to alleviate pressure on your body. Here are some well-known techniques to in essence unwind:

Breathing exercises
• Dynamic muscle recreation
• Exercise

Loosen up Soundly and Earnestly

Your excursion of strain comprises of your examinations and emotions. You could also believe that you are unable to sufficiently deal with the stressors you are confronting (thought), and experience dread (feeling) subsequently, which can go with and even sustain your pressure reaction. Regularly, reconsidering your musings can assist you with relaxing inwardly.

The going with can help you with bettering distance your considerations and interchange this cycle as you make feel of how to relax up as you face your stressors:

• Change your poor self-acknowledgment with high caliber

• Figure out how to reutilize your bits of knowledge so the way where you see sensible stressors for an awesome period is ceaselessly pleasant and substantially less troubling

• Make sense of what your outline mutilations are, for example, win sizeable or bust reasoning, overgeneralizing, making a hurried judgment, concentrating on the negative, naming, and "should" declarations, along these lines as to how to handle them

• Work to create more prominent positive thinking

Step by Step Instructions to Keep up with Unwinding

When you have discovered how to loosen up, you have to unearth less in normal weight. The consequent stage is making sense of how to keep up a state of loosening up and making sense of how to release up again surprisingly after you oversee future stressors. Adding key features to your method for presence can help you with gathering more effects for overseeing stressors you face, and develop to be less open to these stressors too.

The accompanying can assist you with making a lifestyle that reasons you to loosen up and all the more noteworthy productively manage the dread of life:

• Make endeavors to carry on with a low-stress way of life, for example, picking up breathing activities, doing normal exercise, reflecting, writing in a diary, and developing connections

- Learn how to be all the more genuinely flexible.

Targeted Muscle Group Relaxation Script

Progressive muscle relaxation is an action that releases up your mind and body by progressively stressing and relaxation muscle packs all through your entire body. You will tense each muscle pack excitedly, anyway without pushing, and a short time later unexpectedly release the strain and feel the muscle loosen up.

You will tense each muscle for around 5 seconds. If you have any misery or uneasiness at any of the concentrated on muscle social occasions do not waver to block that movement. All through this movement, you may envision the muscles stressing and a surge of relaxation spilling over them as you release that weight. It is huge that you keep breathing all through the movement. Now, let us begin.

Start by finding an agreeable position either sitting or resting in an area where you will not have interfered.

Enable your consideration regarding center just around your body. On the off chance that you start to see your mind meandering, take it back to the muscle you are taking a shot at.

Take a full breath through your stomach area, maintain for a couple of seconds, and breathe out gradually. Once more, as you inhale see your stomach is rising and your lungs loading up with air.

As you exhale out, envision the weight in your constitution being liberated and spilling out of your body.

In addition, again inhale…..and inhale out. Feel your body formally loosening up.

As you experience each movement, make positive to continue relaxing.

Presently, we should begin.

Fix the muscle tissue in your sanctuary by lifting your eyebrows as high as could reasonably be expected. Hold for around 5 seconds. Additionally, release feeling that weight falls away.

Presently stop for cycle 10 seconds.

By and by, smile extensively, feeling your mouth and cheeks tense. Hold for around

5 seconds, and release, esteeming the non-abrasiveness in your face.
Presently delay for cycle 10 seconds.
Next, reclamation your eye muscle tissues by methods for squinting your eyelids immovably shut. Hold for around 5 seconds, and release.
Presently delay for cycle 10 seconds.
Gently pull your head again as despite the fact that to look at the rooftop. Hold for around 5 seconds, and release, feeling the pressure relaxing perpetually.
Presently stop for around 10 seconds.
By and by feeling the greatness of your casual head and neck sink.
Inhale... and out.
In... and out.
Give up all the pressure
In... and out.
By and by, immovably, yet alongside focusing on, grasp your grip fingers and hold this situation until I kingdom to stop. Hold for around 5 seconds, and release.
Presently delay for cycle 10 seconds.
By and by, flex your biceps. Feel that improvement of strain. You may likewise

even imagine that muscle fixing. Hold for around 5 seconds, and release, getting an expense out of that sentiment of obesity.

Inhale in...and out.

By and by reestablishing your triceps by method for expanding your palms out and blasting your elbows. Hold for cycle 5 seconds, and release.

Presently stop for cycle 10 seconds.

Presently marginally raise your shoulders up just as they should contact your ears. Hold for around 5 seconds, and hurriedly discharge them, feeling their weight unwind.

Hold this for around 10 seconds.

Tense your upper returned through moving your shoulders back endeavoring to reach. Hold for around 5 seconds, and afterward discharge.

Postponement for cycle 10 seconds.

Fix your chest with the guide of taking a full breath in, keep up for cycle 5 seconds, and inhale out, covering all the strain.

Directly reclamation the bulk in your tummy by means of sucking in. Hold for cycle 5 seconds, and after that discharge.

Presently relax up for around 10 seconds.

Carefully bend your lower back. Hold for around 5 seconds, loosen up.

Presently release up for around 10 seconds.

Feel the relaxation in your chest spot giving up the pressure and stress, keep up for cycle 5 seconds, and loosen up.

Fix your back end. Hold for around 5 seconds…, release, and imagine your hips falling free.

Presently relax up for cycle 10 seconds.

Fix your thighs by methods for pressing your knees together, as despite the fact that you were holding a penny between them. Hold for cycle 5 seconds… and release.

Presently unwind for around 10 seconds.

By and by flexing your feet, pulling your toes toward you and feeling the strain in your calves. Hold for around 5 seconds, and loosen up, sense the largeness of your legs sinking down.

Presently release up for around 10 seconds.

Turn your toes beneath stressing your feet. Hold for cycle 5 seconds, release.

Presently relax up for cycle 10 seconds.

By and by, imagine a surge of recreation logically spreading through your physical make-up beginning at your head and going directly down to your feet.

Feel the heaviness of your casual body.

Breathe in... and out... in... out....in... out.

Relaxation and Physical Hypnosis Meditation

A wide collection of quintessential cures certifications to improve prosperity by turning in unwinding. A few people utilize the fulfilled country to improve scholarly change. Others experience advancement, stretches, and breathing exercises. Unwinding and "stress the officials" are found to a limited recognition inside the trendy remedial practice. They are fused here in light of the fact that they are much of the time no longer all around brief in typical remedial instructive bundles and because of the cowl with other, all the more noteworthy unquestionably indispensable, medicines.

Hypnosis

Hypnosis is the enrollment of a significantly slackened scholarly state, with duplicated suggestibility and suspension of principal assets. Once in this express, a portion of the time alluded to as a rest instigating trance; sufferers are given helpful recommendations to stimulate changes in propensities or lightening of symptoms. For example, in treatment to end smoking, a hypnosis master may likewise exhort that the influenced individual will in no way, shape or form again discover smoking satisfying or fundamental. Hypnosis for a patient with joint hurt may moreover involve a proposal that the torment can be turned down like the volume of a radio.

A couple of experts use hypnosis as a manual for psychotherapy. The preparation is that in the spellbound express, the perceptive character presents fewer limits to a convincing psychotherapeutic examination, inciting a quickened probability of mental learning. Unwinding and contemplation strategies

One genuinely comprehended instance of a rest way is alluded to distinctively as dynamic muscle unwinding, precise muscle unwinding, and Jacobson unwinding. The influenced individual sits without trouble in a peaceful room.

The person of interest by then tenses many muscles, for instance, these in the correct arm holds the choking for 15 seconds, and at that factor releases it while breathing out. After a brief rest, this affiliation is repeated with another relationship of muscles. In a purposeful way, genuine muscle social events are contracted, by then allowed to loosen up. Deliberately, an assortment of courses of action of the muscle is united. Patients are encouraged to see the complexities among stress and unwinding.

The Mitchell system comprises of grasping places of the body that are reverse to those related with anxiety (fingers spread rather than palms held, for example).

In autogenic planning, patients main focus on experiencing substantial sensations, for instance, warmness and hugeness, in an assortment of bits of their our bodies in a prepared gathering. Different strategies empower the utilization of diaphragmatic breathing that includes profound and moderate stomach breathing combined with a cognizant endeavor to relinquish pressure during exhalation.

Portrayal and imagery procedures incorporate the acknowledgment of a casual kingdom sought after by method for the enhancement of a visual picture, for instance, a sublime scene that improvements the sentiment of unwinding. These photographs would potentially be made by method for the influenced individual or proposed by methods for the master. With regards to this loosening up setting, patients can likewise envision themselves adapting all the more successfully to the stressors in their lives.

Judo or Tai Chi is a fragile game plan of exercises that originates from China. The best-acknowledged mannequin is the "solo structure," a movement of moderate and direct inclines that seek after a set model. It is expressed to upgrade quality, parity, and scholarly serenity. Qigong (explained "chi kung") is another conventional Chinese game plan of helpful exercises. Experts show reflection, physical advancements, and breathe exercises to improve the movement of Qi, the Chinese articulation for body essentialness.

The Process of Hypnosis Using Relaxation and Meditation

In hypnosis, sufferers, as a rule, view experts aside from every individual else's enter for a course of hourly or half-hourly sessions. Some wide experts and other therapeutic specialists use hypnosis as a thing of their all-inclusive logical work and seek after an increasingly drawn-out initial talk with general 10-15-minute courses of action. Patients can be given a post-entrancing idea that enables them to induce self-hypnosis after the treatment course is done. A couple of specialists incorporate pack hypnosis, treating up to twelve patients at some random minute— for example, showing self-hypnosis to numerous people as getting ready for work.

Unwinding and Reflection Procedures

Most releasing up frameworks require systematic exercise to flabbergast. A blend of courses of action for teaching slackening up and reflection exist, including planning also as individual sessions. Releasing up can be skilled in 1 session by planning and sound taping a relaxing up session. Utilizing the sound tape, patients would then have the option to rehearse the systems day through the day at home. Techniques, for instance, dynamic muscle loosening up are definitely not hard to learn; yoga, kendo, and reflection can set aside a long effort to accomplish completely.

Most unwinding methods are pleasant, and numerous solid people practice them without having specific medical issues. Unwinding classes can likewise play a social capacity.

Not at all like in numerous other corresponding treatments, do experts of unwinding methods make analyzations.

They may utilize customary determinations as depicted by the patient to tailor the endorsed program's suitability. Much of the time, nevertheless, the strategy for treatment does not rely upon an exact conclusion.

Helpful Scope

The essential utilization of hypnosis and unwinding methods are for tension, the issue with a solid mental part, (for example, asthma and outbursts of anger), and conditions that can be adjusted by levels of excitement, (for example, torment). They are additionally ordinarily utilized in projects to pressure the senses.

Research evidence

Discoveries from randomized controlled preliminaries bolster the utilization of different unwinding strategies for treating both intense and endless agony, in spite of the fact that two other proposals suggest that methodologic defects may determine the dependability of these discoveries. Randomized preliminaries have demonstrated hypnosis is important for patients with asthma and bad-tempered inside disorder, yoga is useful for patients with asthma, and kendo decreases the fall and anxiety of falling in old individuals. Proof from methodical audits demonstrates hypnosis and unwinding procedures are likely no real advantage to when it comes to smoking cessation, treating hypertension or controlling substance abuse.

Conclusion

You have reached the end of this guide. The next step is to stop reading and to get started practicing mindfulness meditation, or the others meditations (choose what you feel more suitable for you), as frequently as possible. While initially, you may not feel as though you are getting very much out of the time that you put in, the more you keep at it, the more quickly the positive benefits of being mindful are going to start stacking up. Don't get discouraged if at first, you find that your mind remains unruly; every moment you spend fully engrossed at the moment will make it easier to reach the desired mental state in the future. Take it one step at a time, and you will soon find yourself fully engaged in the present without even trying.

www.ingramcontent.com/pod-product-compliance
Lightning Source LLC
Chambersburg PA
CBHW071831080526
44589CB00012B/984